The
Politics
of HOPE

REVIVING THE
DREAM OF DEMOCRACY

DONNA ZAJONC

Political Leadership Coach

A Guide to Political Renewal for Our Times

ISBN 0-9747644-8-5

1st printing July, 2004
2nd printing November, 2004

Published by
Synergy Books
2525 West Anderson Lane
Suite 540
Austin, Texas 78757

Cover Design by Lori Fulsaas
Interior Book Design by Shannon McCafferty

p. 4 Wizard of Id comic strip reprinted by permission of John L. Hart, FLP, and
Creators Syndicate, Inc.

Contents

Acknowledgments

I am deeply grateful for my extraordinary editor, Ceci Miller (see CeciBooks.com) who skillfully mined The Politics of Hope from my life stories and passions. Ceci, you are truly gifted and I thank you dearly for holding my hand while gently nudging me forward.

Thank you, David Womeldorff, for your dazzling insights and loving encouragement. Your positive outlook keeps me going. It was through your brilliant inspiration that I discovered the idea of applying evolutionary concepts to the world of modern politics. I am so grateful for you.

For Jerilyn Brusseau and Rae Cheney who first listened to my desire to write a book and speak professionally about a new type of conscious political leader, I appreciate you so much! In addition to Jerilyn and David, the other members of my Board of Collaborators, Victoria Castle, Bob Linz, David Hager and Carol Winkler: thank you for listening and encouraging me to write. You have been an essential part of my "political habitat." I appreciate Dennis Carlson, Libba Pinchot, Karen Haig, and Alice Tawresey whose sound advice and editing was very valuable, and I'm grateful for Linda Fullerton's new twist on the word *gossip*. Thank you, Debbie Craig, for your many years of insightful feedback and encouragement. To longtime friends Mark and Sheri Bocci, thanks for just being wonderful and dear people. Thank you, Mary Fellows for your friendship and to Dave and Lynn Frohnmayer, thank you for your ethical and kind example of leadership.

To my lifelong spiritual buddies Lani O'Callaghan and

Lynn-Marie Jackson, thank you for your continued love. Those original meetings and our study group were what first gave me hope. To the Sisters of the Holy Names of Jesus and Mary, especially the Leadership Team of Sisters Lynda Thompson, Jane Hibbard and Mary Breiling, thank you for so beautifully demonstrating spiritual collaboration. You and all the Sisters are a gift to humanity.

A special note of gratitude to Molly Gordon, Lisa Mallett, Peggy Joyce, Jan Berg and Cindy Reinhardt who coached me through rediscovering and acting on my passion for public service. You are all awesome coaches!

To my dear children McKenzie, Morgan, and Carson, thank you for your steadfast patience and love as Mom continued to write and sometimes let you fend for yourselves. You three are a gift to our future. Special appreciation and love to my parents Joe and Lois Brownsberger, who first modeled community involvement and servant leadership to me. This book is dedicated to you.

Introduction

I wrote this book because I have hope for the political future of democracy and because of a burning desire to share what I have learned by applying the principles of evolution to politics. The laws of evolution tell us that when a breakdown occurs, new breakthroughs appear. That is what is happening in our nation, and throughout the world, right now. Viewed in this way, our broken political systems are an indication of progress. Far from being defeated, we are drawing closer than ever to our primary aim of true democratic government. When the old systems don't work anymore, we have reason for hope and celebration, for it is then that we begin to envision, just over the horizon, a new and ennobled political future. The fact that we are involved in a process of evolution is what propels individuals, nations and whole cultures to move steadily from what doesn't work toward what works very well. A critical mass or "tipping point" of our citizenry now understands this revelation. We know that the leadership styles which worked in the past cannot lead us successfully through the chaos and complexity of the 21st-century global society.

This awareness inspired me to apply evolutionary thinking to politics. Part One of *The Politics of Hope* outlines the Four Stages of Evolutionary Politics from the first stage of leadership, Anarchy, to the fourth Stage, the Politics of Hope, which emphasizes collaboration and partnership.

We are moving away from heroic styles of leadership in

business, non-profits, families, and neighborhoods, but we have been slow to adopt new models of leadership in the political arena. For this reason the Four Stages of Political Evolution included in this book have been helpful to my clients and seminar participants: political candidates and other public leaders. Examining the Four Stages gives a broader perspective on our current political conflicts and offers a glimpse of the new form of leadership we will need in the future. The move to a more collaborative model of shared leadership and shared responsibility will require the effort of the many, rather than only the few. Part II of this book, "Seven Practices for Becoming a Conscious Public Leader," is designed to help you develop a personal plan of action.

I have an abiding faith in the inherent goodness of our free and open political system. I believe we will emerge from our current trials with a clearer and more dynamic vision for the future.

Whether or not you ever decide to seek public office, I hope that you will acknowledge the inner stirring to participate. With all our foibles and flaws, we are still a country based upon freedom of choice. As citizens, we possess the opportunity to participate in our society and government according to our individual wishes. We have the power to take a creative public role in our country's future—be it on a local, state, or national stage— and in this way we can have a decidedly positive impact on the world at large. I hope that, like me, you will challenge the fear that says, "It's us against them," by replacing it with hope and trust in humanity's innate greatness. When we align ourselves with the highest principles (just as the founders of our country did, despite all *their* foibles and flaws), courage comes naturally. Committing to these principles in thought and action, we can bring nobility back to politics. Together we can revive the dream of democracy.

Part I

The Four Stages
of Political Evolution

Part 1

1 *Politics* Is a Dirty Word

No pessimist ever discovered the secrets of the stars, or sailed to an uncharted land, or opened a new heaven to the human spirit.

—Helen Keller

You must have opened this book for a reason. Perhaps something is stirring in you, a sense of impending chaos as you witness the radical changes taking place in the world. Maybe you despair that our political system is going the way of the dinosaur. Like so many, you may have begun to acquiesce to the notion that most politicians are self-centered and power-hungry. Maybe you fear that your longing for the return of noble political leaders reveals naïve nostalgia, as childish as a belief in the Tooth Fairy. But maybe, like me, in spite of all your doubts, you feel passionately that America's democratic freedom is a gift that carries with it an honorable responsibility. Maybe you harbor a vision of a better, fairer version of our country. But maybe, like many others, your doubts interfere with your taking action, whispering in your ear that people who run for political office are egotists who don't care one iota about the common good. Whatever your views about the current state of our political malaise, something is stirring, demanding to be heard.

> Maybe, like me, in spite of all your doubts, you feel passionately that America's democratic freedom is a gift that carries with it an honorable responsibility.

Do you dream about getting politically involved, of effecting positive change, but aren't sure how to go about it? Given the current perception of politicians, you may be cautious even about revealing that you have such thoughts. Maybe you stop yourself in your tracks, awash in disillusionment: "Me, a politician? I could never be like them (a sellout). I don't want to have anything to do with this broken system."

I hope that is why you picked up this book. If you feel dissatisfied and confused, uncertain about what is happening to our political system, if you want to explore ways to participate effectively *while staying in alignment with your highest principles,* you have come to the right place.

You may be an elected official who ran for office out of a sincere desire to be a conscious political leader and to uphold right action as a public servant. And now, maybe despite your best efforts, you are drowning in a sea of dysfunctional politics that seems systematically to thwart your best efforts at making a difference. Meanwhile, increasing numbers of the very public you seek to serve are not on your side. The morning paper and the evening news pour out endless gossip about crooked politicians. Comic strips and comedians, as usual, find political leaders an easy target, except that the kidding has taken on a biting edge.

WIZARD OF ID

Given the current stigma, why would anyone want to become a public leader today? Our American system has achieved so many great things in the past two centuries, but the current form of that system has quite definitely gone astray. We know that in the midst of all manner of chaos, fear, and distress, people unanimously wish for trusting relationships, for inspiration and action based upon the collective good. That wishfulness may take the form of deep disillusionment or a sense of urgency or even anger; nevertheless, at the very heart of our desire for positive change is innocent hope. We know that the world is undergoing an unprecedented but inevitable shift toward global community and interdependence, whether or not we know how to meet the change. And no matter how disappointed we may be in our efforts to meet that change so far, we always hope to do better in the future.

> The world is undergoing an unprecedented but inevitable shift toward global community and interdependence, whether or not we know how to meet the change.

Renewing the Nobility of Politics

The word *politics* has become a dirty word to most Americans. I hear from my friends and neighbors that they want nothing to do with politics or politicians. Just the sound of the word *politics* makes them feel sick to their stomachs, evoking visions of corrupt, self-centered, fast-talking, deceivers: the scum of the earth. Or perhaps maybe another phrase, equally unflattering, comes to your mind.

When I tell people that I'm writing a book about American politics I receive looks of bewilderment and dismay. They wonder what has happened to me and why I would waste my time. I know, however, that I am not wasting my time. I am dedicated to participating in a new, greater conversation that revives the dream of American democracy.

I long for a time when our country's political servants are our most trusted allies and our children's heroes. Call me naïve or idealistic if you like, but I believe that I share this yearning with you. I believe that is why you picked up this book. Something inside you insists that we can do better. As leaders of the free world, I believe that we must do better.

In generations past, parents longed for their sons and daughters to grow up to be politicians. I can think of no more telling example of a successful democracy than a society of people who cherish this ideal for their children's future. And though our democracy may be in a state of disrepair, it is far from being a hopeless case. Hope, then, is the reason for this book.

Through a sometimes painful, sometimes confusing, and often exhilarating process, I emerged from a state of resignation and political hopelessness. I renewed my own dream of democracy. Along the way I discovered that our political system mirrors what we have learned about all living organisms. Like the rest of creation, it evolves through predictable evolutionary stages. That awareness, along with my studies of human potential, led me to attempt to describe this evolutionary process. I began to see that politics encompasses all forms of human expression, from the most basic and misguided to the highest and most inspiring. The result is the Four Stages of Political Evolution described in Part One of this book. Each stage represents a station in our growth toward conscious public leadership, the ultimate goal of the Politics of Hope. Considering where we are among these stages of our political evolution lays the foundation for the more important personal work presented in Part Two.

> I believe that our next evolutionary leap toward reviving the dream of democracy will come from the concerted actions of the many, not from one great leader of mythic proportions.

Part Two of this book outlines Seven Essential Practices for Becoming a Conscious Public Leader. In this section you will find ways to begin the personal journey toward your own political involvement, in a form that is natural to you. Applying these Seven Practices can help you get clearer about what matters to you, and can offer valuable insights toward becoming politically involved. Not everyone should run for elected office, of course. In any case, I believe that our next evolutionary leap toward reviving the dream of democracy will come from the concerted actions of the many, not from one great leader of mythic proportions. That old leadership paradigm is quickly dying. It is the engagement of the many that will renew our democratic ideals and lead us through the 21st century with wisdom. How you become involved in renewing our democracy—whether as a social activist, a community leader, an elected public servant, a philanthropist, or in some other form— your personal contribution is essential to reviving the dream.

Whenever I am told that there's no hope of changing the American political system, I think about my daughter's favorite sport: soccer. Only 20 years ago, soccer was relatively unknown in our country. Established sports leaders considered it unlikely to become an American tradition. Today there are professional men's and women's soccer leagues all over the nation, and the term *soccer moms* is a line item on every political poll to determine the attitudes of an entire new generation of women. In the same way, surprising new political developments occur every day in all areas of our culture.

What Is a Conscious Public Leader?

I use the term *conscious public leader* throughout this book. While my frame of reference often springs from personal experiences during my time in elected public service, I intend the term to include all forms of public leadership. This may be community leadership in various non-profit organizations, neighborhood associations, social activist groups, or political organizations.

I have a strong belief that our leadership models are undergoing a radical transformation. We are rapidly moving away from hierarchical, domination-centered forms of leadership toward a more open, collaborative model. Such a shift requires, even demands, that the many, rather than the few, share the role of leadership. Reviving the dream of democracy requires the full participation of a massive number of citizens. Without interest and action by the many, democracy's future will remain in peril.

A conscious political leader is one who is fully conscious, who has awakened to the value of and fully embraces collaboration as the ideal working model of leadership. While conscious public leaders may vary in overall style, they share an unswerving intention to govern in service of the collective good.

Our Broken Political System

By all measurements, our American political system is broken. As many as 40 percent of American adults do not vote in national elections, and in off year, statewide elections about 65 percent of the electorate stays home. In 1960 almost 63 percent of voting-age adults went to the polls to choose between John Kennedy and Richard Nixon. In 1996, after a steady decline in voter turnout, 48.9 percent of voting-age Americans chose among Bill Clinton, Bob Dole, and H. Ross Perot.

Americans are less involved in their civic affairs today than in the past two decades and it shows up in many different ways. Over the last two decades, the number of office seekers in any year at all levels in the American body politic—from school boards to city council—shrank by 15 percent. According to Robert Putnam, in his best selling book *Bowling Alone*, this means that Americans lost more than a quarter of a million candidates per year from which they could have chosen at the voting booths. Putnam and his staff analyzed the Roper data on social and political trends and found that, between 1973 and 1994, the number of Americans who attended even one public meeting on city or school affairs in the previous year had fallen by 40 percent. Over the same two decades, the ranks of those who had served as an officer or a committee member for a local club or organization had thinned by an identical

> Many citizens now view any form of political involvement as an exercise in futility.

40 percent. Over these 20 years, the number of members of "some group interested in better government" fell by one-third.

Many citizens believe that the American system has gone hopelessly awry, and view any form of political involvement as an exercise in futility. Roughly 30 percent of Americans have declined to join political parties, registering instead as Independents. Americans are avoiding political involvement at all levels, in numbers never before imagined.

Is it any wonder that so many Americans have rejected the current political conversation? Political pundits and spin doctors annoy us with endless analysis of minutiae, focusing on details of the candidates' campaign strategies rather than the meat of their message.

I am not suggesting that we dismantle media coverage of political campaigns. Media campaigns, GOTV (get out the vote) programs, fundraising, volunteer recruitment, and psychological techniques are part and parcel of our democratic election process. Nevertheless, it will all be in vain if leaders do not begin to recognize the American public's impatience with phony communication.

A Heritage of Hope

America's democratic heritage is built upon hope. Optimism, pursuit of happiness, and individual freedom form the core of our nation's political philosophy. If we lose hope, we lose our identity as Americans. But hope for what? Our dream of democracy is rooted in the past. That past served us very well in building upon our parents' desires and the desires of their parents before them, at a time when our world was an altogether different place. The rapidly changing global society in which we now find ourselves presents fresh challenges, new questions, that cannot be resolved by traditional means.

Is there anything more devastating than feeling hopeless? In the midst of all our experience, the human spirit has an unlimited ability to face any obstacle as long as there is hope. Certainly anger, fear, and grief exist, as do all the other emotions that make life unbearable at times. But as long as there is hope, our spirit keeps going.

The Politics of Hope is a confident anticipation of our new collective political vision and the ability to make that vision a reality. Hope without vision is lost. It is a waste of energy to live a life filled with narcissistic pleasures, blind to the suffering and needs of others. America, however, is a mature country with mature citizens. By cultivating a mature hope, grounded in present reality, we can begin to evolve into a more inclusive and conscious culture. It is hope that allows us to return to the world of public service with a firm belief in endless possibility.

> Optimism, pursuit of happiness, and individual freedom form the core of our nation's political philosophy. If we lose hope, we lose our identity as Americans.

Applying the model of the Four Stages of Political Evolution renews our hope, as we grasp the idea that our political system is an ever-growing organism. Its unfolding is happening before our very eyes. Because today we are experiencing the American political system in a broken state, it is tempting to believe that this brokenness is permanent. In the physical world we call this the law of inertia: all bodies at rest remain resting. Feeling the inertia of the current state of American politics, we tend to enter a state of hopelessness, believing that nothing will ever change. According to the same laws of nature, however, we have learned that species survive and thrive when they learn to work together, adapt, and support one another. Inertia isn't forever. Our democracy will grow and expand and ultimately break through to a new stage when we learn how to live and work collaboratively.

It is my hope that by examining the Four Stages of Political Evolution you will feel inclined to participate in the Politics of Hope, which in turn will attract others who dare to believe in reviving the dream of democracy. It will take a great number of us to reinvigorate America. Our faith may be tested in the process because we do not yet know what this new, rejuvenated version of American democracy will look like. We recognize that what we have known, despite its inherent greatness, will not work in our new world. As in nature, the ineffective is dying and attempting to create itself anew. In this sense, there is really nothing wrong with where we are right now as a democracy. Every beneficial change is preceded by a period of discomfort and awkwardness. We are uncomfortable now, and our politics feel awkward. We might just as soon give up, except that hope calls us to go further and to reach higher, to elevate humanity.

If we will follow the laws of nature, the law of evolution that urges us forward, we must engage ourselves in the hard work of first learning who we are, and then focusing our efforts on becoming who we want to become.

2

The Four Stages of Political Evolution

The greatest of all laws is the law of progressive development. Under it, in the wide sweep of things, people grow wiser as they grow older, and societies better.

—Christian Bovee

I believe that we live in a unique time in history, in a unique country that, at its core, is founded on freedom and opportunity. I also believe that something is terribly wrong. So many of us harbor the same private secret: we love our country and want to be part of an enlightened society, and yet feel a little guilty about turning inward toward home, family, and private desires while shelving our concerns about a broader cultural transformation. Physicists have even managed to prove that our world is expanding, growing, and evolving, and yet everywhere we turn the old systems we used to rely on appear to be breaking down. Where do we place our faith, our precious time, our vision and personal energy, in order to assist the collective good? What to do? Where to start?

I believe, as you may, that this is a time of opportunity. I want to affirm the hopeful opportunities that exist for you to participate in getting the people's business done. Many people know that our global community is on the verge of a breakthrough. The future systems that will emerge from that breakthrough are as yet unknown; however, one thing is clear: conscious public leaders must begin to prepare themselves for that new day. To doggedly maintain the political status quo in the face of the world's need for innovative thought and creative alliances to solve our shared problems is to court disaster. Even though at this moment we may not know what form our political participation will take in our country's ever more rapidly unfolding future, the time to prepare is *now*.

Throughout this book I will be discussing the Four Stages of Political Evolution that we as Americans are destined to move through in order to revive our democracy. As these Stages unfold in our awareness and in our surroundings, we will gain an increasingly clear view of how to enliven our participation in our political system. I understand that for many citizens, our current system appears irrelevant, and the word *politics* does nothing toward drawing them to public service. However, an evolution is taking place that will transform both our system of government and our forms of participation in it. For this reason I am suggesting that we cultivate a radical new level of patience and steadiness, to prepare ourselves for new opportunities that none of us can, as yet, fully appreciate. It is essential for our most dedicated and mature citizens (you and I) to maintain a sense of possibility and freedom, and to make that freedom real by contemplating public service.

Such preparation is a uniquely personal kind of search. As a political leadership coach, I develop tools to help my clients understand their deepest reasons for running for office. One such overarching tool is an awareness of the Four Stages of Political Evolution. Understanding of these four stages provides a model to help tame our confusion by pointing us toward ever higher levels of awareness and conscious leadership.

> An evolution is taking place that will transform both our system of government and our forms of participation in it.

The mind, by nature, both takes comfort and feels disquieted when it is engaged in a process of growth and expansion. When we see that process more clearly, we can choose the stage of growth we aspire to.

Harnessing Chaos, Adapting to Change

The Arlington Institute, a futurist think-tank group located in Washington DC, recently issued a statement about our future and the radical global changes we face in the next two decades.

> *We are now living in a period of significant transition—a foreshortened span of time, during which our surroundings and experiences will change more than during any era in history. Humanity has never lived through the convergence of global forces now in play. During the next two decades, almost every aspect of life will be fundamentally reshaped.*

The American democratic system is involved in an early stage of transformation similar to the birth of our nation—the American Revolution of the 18th century. This new revolution will be fundamentally different, however. Complex cultural, environmental, and economic issues around the globe, technologies of high-speed communication and mass destruction, as well as the ever-growing gap between the wealthy and the world's poor are situations that call for a new breed of public leader.

Notice the last sentence of the Arlington statement: "During the next two decades, almost every aspect of life will be fundamentally reshaped." When we really digest the magnitude of change that is taking place in our lives, it becomes obvious that our leaders must possess unprecedented levels of improvisational adaptability and creativity. They must be visionaries. Successful public servants are conscious of their motives to serve and have sought to develop their own inner spiritual philosophy. Having delved into their personal virtues, they seek to expand them, to keep their minds open to new possibilities, and to act in service of their principles rather than in service of a personal agenda. Servant leaders know that only by consciously living in simple alignment with timeless principles of commonsense fairness and integrity, will they be empowered to make their best public contribution.

Wherever we look, it is readily apparent that the new quantum speed of life impacts all areas of our world. Our younger generations have, in effect, collapsed: changes that once took a generation to accomplish now take place within only a few years. My 23-year-old daughter did not use the Internet until she was a sophomore in high school, while my 18-year-old daughter was online in the sixth grade, with 200 people in her chat room! Though they were born only five years apart, my two daughters have grown up in almost entirely different "generations." The result of so much rapid technological advancement in such a short span of time is that leaders within different age groups possess dramatically different frames of reference. If we seek to reinvigorate our country's greatness, we must attract leaders who understand how to bring together groups with divergent world views, leaders who remain steady of heart and mind through the changing times in which we are living.

> The success of American democracy over the next century is dependent upon our ability to attract a vast new community of conscious public leaders.

I believe that the success of American democracy over the next century is dependent upon our ability as a society to attract a vast new community of conscious public leaders who will lead us wisely through the chaos of the 21st century.

Conscious public leaders seek first to know themselves. They have discovered their unique gifts and have made a decision to share those gifts with the world. This book urges you, too, to reflect on your calling, to unearth your passions and become fully in touch with your own qualities of servant leadership. Whether or not you put those qualities to use in public office, you can change your internal questions from "What if?" and "Why me?" to "How can I be of service?" and "What can I offer that will improve the situation?" Changing the internal conversation you have with yourself brings transformative power to the conversations you have with others as well. And that is the beginning of conscious public leadership.

We in American society also face a choice: whether to resist our collective fears or, as a culture, to face them head-on in order to fully realize our greatness. Fear is as old as the hills; we all experience it. The most crippling fear of all is that which keeps us from living our deepest desires. Great public leaders experience the same fear that the rest of us feel. The difference is this: they push through their fear by knowing that they serve a higher purpose than their own ends. This knowledge gives them the courage to serve.

American Poet Laureate William Stafford wrote, "What you fear will not go away. It will take you into itself and bless you and keep you." Our fears become gifts to ourselves when we are willing to see the present. The reward of consciousness is clarity of choice and the natural satisfaction that comes from identifying our fears and acting on the growth-inducing challenges they bring to bear on our character. If we resist and struggle against our fears, we may as well be asleep. Given free reign, fear will sabotage our highest goals, our most favorable opportunities.

Conscious public leaders have made the leap from their individual interests to the well-being of the whole. Sounds wonderful in theory. But how can we live our principles in a way that helps create globally beneficial political policy? It is an ever-evolving challenge. The new breed of political leaders will focus on setting aside their personal fears, offering their time and resources in service of a purpose they may or may not see fulfilled during their lifetime: transforming our political system for the sake of generations to come.

Fear is magnified by chaos; conscious public leaders are fully aware that fear grows during chaotic times. They also take comfort in knowing that evolution occurs one step at a time. Human systems are not static but fluid, always forging new patterns. The emergence of ever more complex systems in this time of quantum change makes leadership, decision-making, and implementation of policy an increasingly intricate art form. For this reason, the Four Stages of Political Evolution can help us look into where we are now and where we are going.

The Four Stages of Political Evolution

Living in the midst of global transformation is only frightening if we never pause to observe the evolutionary stages of political development we are traversing. If we look at the big picture, we can transcend our fears. We can make the move to hope and trust, and begin to envision—and to consciously participate in—our personal evolution through these stages of political activity.

Each of the Four Stages represents a complex mix of cultural, societal, and psychological influences. An individual may demonstrate characteristics of each of the Four Stages. My purpose here is not to analyze the observed behaviors and thinking patterns that characterize each political stage; such is the work of sociologists and political scientists, and I am neither. Rather, I want to explore with you how individuals move through these stages to become powerful and conscious public leaders for the good of all. In other words, I am interested in getting to Stage Four: the Politics of Hope. What will nudge the politically unengaged—many of whom are currently operating in Stage Three Resignation—to rejoin the political conversation as public leaders? How can leaders who now operate out of a fear-based view of power politics begin to appreciate the interconnectedness of our global society? The purpose of this book is to question ourselves deeply and to examine the status quo for cracks, so that together we can lay a firm foundation for the future of American democracy.

Based upon the work of Elisabeth Kubler-Ross, M. Scott Peck, Erik Erikson, Robert Kegan, Ken Wilber, Stephen Covey, Don Beck, and other anthropological researchers and philosophers, I have adapted stages of community and spiritual and human development to describe how we are moving toward a more enlightened political future. The result is the Four Stages of Political Evolution: (1) Anarchy, (2) Traditionalism, (3) Resignation, and (4) Conscious Public Leadership, or the Politics of Hope.

The behaviors, assumptions, and characteristics outlined below are based on my 30 years of experience in politics, on my study of the new models of leadership and community, and on alternative medical research regarding the mind/body/spirit connection. Much of what I observe and assert here also stems from my experience as an elected politician. The Four Stages model allows me to explain to my political leadership coaching clients what is happening in the political milieu and why it is happening. It describes the phases of political involvement that each person exhibits according to her level of awareness, her motives, and her desire to service the collective good. In this way, the Four Stages can help us think past the current limitations of our democracy, so that we may grow and live in greater awareness of the vast range of mystery that confronts us all as citizens.

> The purpose of this book is to question ourselves deeply and to examine the status quo for cracks, so that together we can lay a firm foundation for the future of American democracy.

Stage One: Anarchy

Stage One Qualities

Community connectedness nonexistent
Hopelessness and rage
Incapable of living in service to others
Only concerned for one's individual welfare
Lacking integrity, honesty, guiding principles
Rationalizing violence, acts that harm others are "necessary"
Strong fundamentalist belief system that denies all other possibilities

Stage One Assumptions

All actions are justifiable if they serve personal self-interest
All government is inherently evil and limits the rights of individuals

Stage One Examples

Skinheads and KKK
Timothy McVeigh
Abortion clinic attackers

Stage Two: Traditionalism

Stage Two Qualities

Politics of fear and polarization
"Us vs. Them," "black or white" thinking that always makes the
    other wrong
Dogmatic and simplistic answers to complex questions
Look for strong political leader who will save us
Rigid adherence to party line
Want leaders to remove the chaos and fix the problem
Either "for us or against us"

Stage Two Assumptions
To accomplish anything, a leader must dominate and manipulate others
Anyone who does not agree with us is wrong, possibly dangerous
Winning means defeating and beating down others
Short-term goals are more important than long-term vision
Management gets paid to think and labor gets paid to do
Cannot get anything accomplished unless your team wins
Longing for the "good old days"
Change is something to be managed and controlled
Voters can't handle the truth
Human beings are evil and must be controlled by guilt and secrets
People enter into religion to escape mystery and chaos

Stage Two Examples
Republicans vs. Democrats
Labor vs. Management
Urban vs. Rural
Federal vs. State
Men vs. Women
Rush Limbaugh vs. Michael Moore
Short-term quarterly business profits vs. long-term sustainable growth

Stage Three: Resignation

Stage Three Qualities
Aware of possibilities within our free and democratic political
   system, yet resigned that the traditional system has no
   relevance to their lives
Dropped out of political systems, inactive in political parties,
   feel politically powerless

Vote sporadically, if at all

Values-centered life based on inner spirituality, psychology, and service

Make daily life choices in accord with ecological values

Stage Three Assumptions

American democracy is based upon the individual power, wealth, and special interests of those in office

Our democratic system has lost its greatness

Politicians will do anything to get elected; their interests are on behalf of their contributors, not the collective good

American traditional political system is irrelevant to modern realities

We can affect only the lives of our immediate families and neighborhoods

Organizing through non-profits, churches, and non-governmental organizations is the only way to affect real change

Globalization is a powerful force; our country now lacks the vision and support to lead the world

Deepening their spirituality, yet still struggling with how to apply their spiritual and religious life in our modern global world

Stage Three Examples

Tend to not be organized into a cohesive movement; have short term, ad hoc response to specific needs or issues

Growing number of non-profit organizations

Some philanthropic foundations

Home-schooling

Some social activists

Stage Four: Politics of Hope

Stage Four Qualities

Use collaborative action as pathway to solutions

Form new alliances across old political boundaries

Speak and act with integrity, honesty, and inspiration

Have done significant inner spiritual work and speak openly and authentically

Aspire to act and serve from higher motives of service and generosity

Define today's political vision in light of future needs

Use personal power to activate greatness in others

Comfortable with change, chaos, and complexity

Stage Four Assumptions

It is important to maintain hope and optimism in times of chaos, fear, and conflict

Understands the interconnectedness of all things

Power is used to motivate and inspire rather than dominate and control others

Our culture will continue to experience rapid change; embracing the chaos is one of the great challenges for all public servants

Every human being wants to hear and know the truth

Has made a conscious choice to participate in politics and social activism that helps the electorate understand the chaotic forces at play in our society today

True leadership integrates paradoxes: power with gentleness, destiny with luck, certainty with mystery

Our future depends on respecting our global interdependence

Has a highly developed religious and/or spiritual practice that respects all paths, and which guides social and political activism

Stage Four Examples

Mahatma Gandhi

Nelson Mandela

Dalai Lama

Dr. Martin Luther King, Jr.

Early Founders of American Democracy

Conversation Cafés and Let's Talk America

King County Republican Councilwoman Kathy Lambert and King County Democratic Councilwoman Julia Patterson, co-sponsoring the "De-publican" fundraiser in Seattle, August 2003

As a nursing student, I remember reading Erik Erickson's stages of human development with great appreciation. Each stage is based upon principles of human potential that must be fully realized before the human being evolves into the next stage of development. Erickson's stages of life are based upon patterns and cycles that emerge in all that we do. If we apply those stages to our political development, we can better understand how conflict arises when we interact with other individuals or countries who are acting from a different developmental focal point. As we reach higher levels of consciousness, both individually and in our political conversations, we will create new ways of unlocking our conflicts and using them to forge real alliances.

French philosopher, Catholic Priest, and paleontologist Pierre Teilhard de Chardin spoke to the nature of the evolutionary process and the increasing complexity of systems. He spoke about the direction of evolution toward the convergence of increased complexity and increased consciousness, breaking through to a higher order level of simplicity. The idea that simplicity is waiting on the other side of complexity may be difficult to grasp at first, but Teilhard is telling us that if we continue forward in midst of the fear and chaos by increasing our conscious awareness, we will arrive at an expansive

	STAGE 1	STAGE 2
	Anarchy	**Traditionalism**
Political Point of View	"All authority, political or otherwise, is inherently evil."	"We must defeat the opposing party to do good."
Level of Hope	"There is no hope. Destroy the system."	"Winning is our only hope."
Political Action	Reactive, rebellious	Competitive, dominating, hierarchical, Us vs Them
Emotional Drive	Anger	Fear, Desire to win control
Trust	"Trust no one."	"Trust our candidate to solve our problems."
Service	Serves self alone	Appearance of selfless service masks service of personal ego
Motives	Destroy, disempower government	Elect a leader who will avert chaos, fix our problems
Power	Power against others at any cost Lose/Lose	Power *over* others Win/Lose
Truth/ Communication	"Truth is relative." (Believe no one)	"The public can't handle the truth." (Information must be spun or withheld)

STAGE 3	STAGE 4	
Resignation	**Politics of Hope**	
"Politics is irrelevant to our lives, not a source of good."	"Politics is a vehicle to create alliances with others for common good."	**Political Point of View**
"Politics is hopeless. We must create an oasis/ shelter in private life."	"Where there is integrity, there is hope."	**Level of Hope**
Neutral, disengaged	Collaborative, inspirational	**Political Action**
Resignation, depression	Love, respect, trust in goodness	**Emotional Drive**
"Trust only yourself and your immediate family and community."	"Trust the evolutionary process and our collective wisdom to create fair policy."	**Trust**
Serves family and local community	True selfless service, based on addressing the needs of "seven generations" hence	**Service**
Preserve values outside politics, acting within local community	Consciously accept role of leadership as a contribution and calling	**Motives**
Personal Power within a limited framework	Power with others Win/win	**Power**
"Truth is rare." (Corporate media is corrupted by political spin)	"Truth is the Essential nature of every human being."	**Truth/ Communication**

simplicity that is all inclusive. Rather than becoming increasingly complex beings, we may become so simple and direct in our principled responses to the problems that face our world community that we create a global breakthrough. We can start now to examine what moves us, what matters to us, and what holds us back, in order to prepare for this new era. We can become conscious public leaders, and we can support conscious public leaders. Whichever direction we take, let us simply begin.

3

The First Two Stages of Political Evolution: Anarchy; Traditionalism

No power is strong enough to be lasting
if it labors under the weight of fear.

—Cicero

Stage One: Anarchy

Anarchists are a complex breed. By definition, *anarchism* (the political theory that all forms of government are incompatible with the individual and social liberty and should be abolished) houses a diverse set of interpreters, each acting in accordance with an individual philosophy. For this reason, Anarchists' political stances and forms of activism vary widely.

Based on the idea that all structures of hierarchical authority are detrimental to the freedoms and potential of each individual, Anarchism asserts that each human being is capable of managing her own affairs through unique gifts and creativity. Ethics are a private matter and should remain outside legal or religious authority. A common theme among Anarchist philosophers is that an individual is responsible for his own behavior.

> Since according to Anarchy all power is corrupt, the Anarchist abhors all power structures.

Anarchists believe that all forms of hierarchical structures, such as government and religious institutions, are abusive authorities—self-perpetuating power structures organized to enrich themselves and their influential constituents at the expense of others. Since according to Anarchy all power is corrupt, the Anarchist abhors all power structures. Anarchy asserts that the authority derived by government robs individuals of their fundamental right to personal and moral decision-making.

To many, the assertions of Anarchy sound similar to the libertarian philosophy that supports minimizing governmental interference in our lives. Libertarians often rely on the survival of the fittest doctrine and staunchly believe in the free enterprise system. Most Anarchists differ with the Libertarian Party on capitalism and free market economies, however: Anarchists want to abolish the current capitalistic economy that, in their eyes, unduly favors huge (and largely unaccountable) private corporations.

The generally accepted view of Anarchy is that any act is justified if it contributes to the overthrow of government or another hierarchical structure. Were the much-publicized sniper attacks on the innocent citizens of Virginia an example of Anarchy? In one form, yes. But some theorists would maintain that an attack upon innocent citizens smacks more accurately of mental illness (or just plain thuggery) than Political Anarchy. While motives for the sniper attacks may not yet be entirely clear, what we do know is that the snipers took the law into their own hands. Most Anarchists today enter the arena of intellectual debate rather than perpetrate violent acts in support of their views. Nonetheless, one does not have to look far to find examples of lawless and violent Anarchist movements.

Anarchists claimed partial responsibility for the French Revolution of the late 1700s and played a large role in the Bolshevik Russian Revolution in the early 1900s. And some would say there was a strong Anarchist leadership at the root of the 1960s anti-war and feminist movements. Violence accompanied many anti-war demonstrations and certainly played a role in the racial wars of the late 1960s. Because it rules out all possibility of working toward a greater good in cooperation with the existing system, Anarchy is antithetical to the Politics of Hope, which depends on creative collaboration by concerned citizens. Anarchy could also be considered the first step in the process of political evolution—it is that trip down a hopeless, dead-end street that, in transformational terms, so often precedes arriving at the right address.

Developing alliances or collaborative relationships across old political boundaries is almost impossible for Anarchists. Any political structure is considered immoral because it is powerful, and the existence of any power, according to Anarchy, means that the individual's rights have been thwarted. It is a stance that communicates frustration and hopelessness. Anarchy rules out consideration for humanity as a whole, since concern for the common good flies in the face of individual rights. When government is assumed to be inherently evil, all forms of cooperation with government are considered destructive. A strong fundamentalist belief system props up the Anarchist's views, prevents open dialogue with all those who disagree, and engenders attachment to communities that are transient in nature.

During my years of legislative service, I did not personally witness Stage One Anarchy behavior. Peaceful demonstrations in front of the State Capitol Building or visiting your friendly legislator were not part of the Anarchist's behavior pattern. So-called eco-terrorist activities began during my days as a legislator, and we treated this activity simply as a clear violation of property laws. Later, when I learned of abortion clinic shootings, I came closest to witnessing Stage One in the evolution of politics.

Stage One Anarchy is relatively rare in America today. The 1995 Oklahoma City bombing by Timothy McVeigh is an apt example. McVeigh exhibited radical, anti-power, anarchic philosophy and acted with violence toward innocent federal workers with the intention of bringing down the governmental apparatus. Abortion clinic attackers—Anarchists with radical fundamentalist religious views—believe that the U.S. Supreme Court's decision protecting women's reproductive rights is immoral, and that the only way to combat the system that allows abortion is to exercise their "individual right" to attack female patients and clinic workers.

It has been estimated that fewer than one percent of Americans align themselves with Anarchic philosophies. But although the number of Stage One Anarchists is relatively small, it is essential to include them as we consider the range of political activity in our society. Like everyone else, Anarchists make a contribution: their views often spark significant philosophical trends in the long term. American revolutionaries who masqueraded as Indians and threw tea into the Boston Harbor were Anarchists. They loudly protested King George's tax, which they saw as unfair, sparking an uprising that later gave way to full-scale revolt by the masses; we now proudly salute them as courageous freedom fighters.

Some of the activists who demonstrated in 1999 on the streets of Seattle, Washington, against the World Trade Organization policies clearly illustrated the principles of Anarchy. A few protesters randomly broke windows and created property damage significant enough to necessitate the closure of many downtown Seattle businesses. While most of the demonstrators conducted themselves peacefully, the few who created mayhem received international attention, forcing the world to focus on the policies of the WTO. Those who fight on behalf of their concerns for the impact of globalization believe that a revolution is in the making, and they are willing to give up their life and liberty to promote laws that support workers, reduce violence and abuse toward child laborers, and dictate clean

> Like everyone else, Anarchists make a contribution: their views often spark significant philosophical trends in the long term.

environmental standards. While their behavior during the WTO Conference was strongly criticized, the international attention these Anarchists brought to WTO policies sparked a debate centered on globalization. In the midst of their chaotic and tumultuous methods of protest, Anarchists are usually seen as fringe reactionaries. But however outrageous their statements and actions seem, in the context of social change they often foreshadow what mainstream America will soon be thinking.

Born of ultimate frustration, terrorist attacks are the most strident form of Anarchy. Terrorists have abandoned all hope of working within the system; violent overthrow of the enemy power structure has become the sole purpose of their lives. Unlike the intellectual and classical anarchic theorists who oppose all power structures, today's international terrorists believe that only their own power structure and belief system should be allowed to exist. Suicide bombers live to kill the enemy and to ignite further conflict. It is through war that terrorists intend to establish their philosophy and culture as dominant.

Attacks by the Al Qaeda network and other international terrorists have been well organized, boasting complex strategic command centers. Unlike snipers, abortion clinic assassins, or the Timothy McVeighs who act alone, international terrorists form militarist-controlled networks that act in concert on command. Unlike classic Anarchists, who are opposed to all power structures and seek to empower the individual, most international terrorists want to replace others' philosophies and civilizations with their own forms. How they are viewed in the world community depends on the culture doing the viewing. As it was with our American revolutionaries, someone branded a *terrorist* in one country is hailed as a *freedom fighter* in another. Through their dramatic and often violent means, Anarchists get the attention of the world. Whether terrorists can successfully communicate their points of view, clarifying the reasons that cause them to resort to violence, remains to be seen.

Invariably frustrated and angry, Anarchists believe that their world view is the only truth; they denounce the rest of the world as blind and immoral. Anarchists are fully engaged, energized, committed, and self-directed. Alliance with fellow Anarchists is often difficult, however, due to their desire to eschew organizations and power structures. Though it may be said that the methods of Anarchy contribute to social change by offering a glimpse of social unrest, Anarchism remains no more than a first step in the evolution of politics, which works always toward creative, inclusive, and respectful collaboration. The Politics of Hope will always, by definition, stretch beyond the parameters of Anarchism, since the philosophy of Anarchy (and its tolerance of violent, lawless, and angry acts) does not support personal or political growth.

> As it was with our American revolutionaries, someone branded a *terrorist* in one country is hailed as a *freedom fighter* in another.

Having said all that, it is important, as we move through the Four Stages of Political Evolution, to understand that we all have parts of each stage within us at any one time and that we may move back and forth between stages. There are certainly times when I feel like an Anarchist, ready to throw a tantrum because I vehemently disagree with a policy. I do not, however, react with violence or a desire to harm others. When we get a speeding ticket, we may be furious at the police officer and feel ready to take the law into our own hands, but most of us don't do it. While we may share some of these feelings, our lives are not possessed by the beliefs and assumptions of Stage One Politics. It is my experience however, that individuals reside primarily in one stage or another, as they navigate their participation through our system of democracy.

Let's move now from Stage One into Stage Two of Evolutionary

Politics. Anarchists feel antagonistic toward Traditionalists who inhabit the second stage because Traditionalists are fully involved in the tightly-knit hierarchy of the American political power system.

Stage Two: Traditionalism

Individuals in Stage Two of Political Evolution are strong proponents of the existing governmental hierarchy. Fully engaged in American politics, Traditionalists participate primarily in the two-party system at the precinct, county, state, and federal levels. They are the people who legislate the rules, the political insiders who dictate the current policies. Traditionalists may be lawmakers themselves or they may obtain access to elected officials by volunteering in campaigns, turn-out-the-vote efforts, phone banks, door-to-door campaigning, raising and donating money, or simply posting a sign on their lawn.

Elected officials are probably the strongest defenders of the Traditionalist power base. It is part of the human condition to want to keep the power and influence one achieves by winning public office. Candidates often campaign for a year or more and learn to thrive within the status quo of the political election system. Once they are elected and have mastered the system and its rules, they are understandably reluctant to change it. Thus the Traditional political system, together with its "us against them" mentality, becomes self-perpetuating; its politicians resist reforms. This resistance to reform constitutes the Achilles' heel of political evolutionary Stage Two Traditionalism: it continually fails to keep up with the natural fluidity of our culture—a characteristic that becomes acutely noticeable in the wake of a dramatic social change.

I mastered the components of a successful Traditionalist

political campaign at an early age. I learned how to bring my name to familiarity, how to raise money, how to attract volunteers, and how to speak publicly. At age 28 my enthusiasm and positive attitude attracted volunteers and voters. On my first try at public office, having lived in my community for only 18 months, I unseated a three-term legislator with 62 percent of the vote. Rarely did I speak about issues. I have an unusual name, and I created enough uproar about how to pronounce my name that our entire campaign consisted of teaching people how to pronounce Zajonc ("Say-John" appeared below my name on all the campaign signs). I heard more clever comments about my unique name than I did about any current issue before the legislature. I was a quick study at the campaign schools I attended. They taught us to avoid issues. "People vote for people, not issues" was the prevailing mantra. Quite early in my political life, I had learned the art of manipulation. As a young woman legislator who now held a seat that had long been occupied by a member of the opposite

> Fully engaged in American politics, Traditionalists are the political insiders who legislate the rules.

political camp, I was considered a rising star in my party. Though I loved the attention, at the same time I was rather dazed and confused. As a political moderate I was often philosophically out of step with my caucus, even though much of what it took to fit in came naturally to me. It didn't escape my notice that the majority leader doled out committee assignments and participated in most of the budget negotiations with the Speaker. I believed that advancing in my party would benefit my career, so in my second term I managed to get appointed Assistant Leader, which allowed me to become involved in many of the leadership discussions.

The feeling of being a little out of my element persisted. As a party leader, I was instructed to do everything possible to help other members of my party get elected. Clearly the only way that

I would someday be Speaker or Chair of the Ways and Means Committee was if my party gained control. In service of this end, I joined a group of legislators who kept track of the voting records of legislators from the opposite party. Then I recruited new candidates to run for office against these legislators. Although I thought that many of them had done a fine job in office, alas, they were members of the wrong party.

At this time in my career, I was deeply engaged in Stage Two Traditionalist politics. To get things done in the only way I understood, I thought I had to win higher office, so I aligned myself with county and state party officials. I did not feel particularly close to the party line, yet I had a firm grip on the "political reality"—or so I thought.

During my third term, in the early 1980s, the anti-nuclear weapons debate had grown particularly intense. One evening a woman well-known for her outspoken opposition to our country's strategic arms race with Russia appeared in a public discussion with a group of concerned citizens. As a legislator who shared her concerns about the increasing proliferation of nuclear warfare, I attended the gathering. Later my name appeared in the paper as one of those who had attended the meeting.

The next morning I was scheduled to have coffee with the vice chairperson of our county party. I had called to enlist her support for my campaign for our party's nomination of Secretary of State. She had arrived at the restaurant ahead of me and already had a cup of coffee. I greeted her warmly, but as I sat down, I noticed that her right hand was so tightly gripped around the coffee cup that her knuckles had gone white. Through clenched teeth she said, "I see you were at the peace rally last night. Are you one of those people who are FOR peace?"

I will always remember that comment. I said softly, "Yes, I am *for* peace." And she replied, "Well, you know what I mean. Are you one of the anti-nuclear people?" I politely indicated my support for a reduction in nuclear arms.

Despite her obvious displeasure with my position, I received my party's nomination for Secretary of State, defeating two gentlemen who were also vying for the position. As it turned out, however, I was much too "liberal" for my party. In the end they ran a third-party candidate with truly conservative credentials, siphoned off substantial percentage points, and helped defeat me in the general election. My story is a classic illustration of Stage Two Traditional politics: for the way that I systematically climbed the ladder of power politics as well as for how my party tossed me out when I proved to be out of step with their views.

Like Anarchists, Traditionalists hold rigid, dogmatic beliefs, but without the phobia against organizational hierarchies. Traditionalists are able to cooperate, as long as the cooperation unwaveringly supports the party line. Political issues are considered in black-and-white terms. My coffeehouse story illustrates how I bumped up against the conservative point of view, but the same rigid thinking exists among Traditionalist liberal interest groups. In my experience, the so-called left wing is often just as ready to criticize, and ostracize, a member who does not jump on their bandwagon 100 percent. Just as conservative political interest groups do, some liberal women's, environmentalist, and labor groups often say, "You're either with us or against us." This black-and-white thinking leaves no room for compromise, for process; no possibility of collaboration to create new solutions to old problems. Traditionalists fall prey to their own limitations in the form of simplistic, polarized thinking, whether they stand at the conservative or the liberal end of the political spectrum.

A Traditional System

Because almost all of the 50 states have laws protecting the two-party system, it is increasingly difficult for a candidate to win a primary election if he does not fully toe the party line. The laws protecting the political parties are based upon closed election systems that grant only party members the right to vote in primaries. The result is obvious. Party nominees are more and more rigid in their points of view. No wonder that upwards of 30 percent of Americans have branded both the Democratic and Republican parties as irrelevant, and register themselves as Independent. Those who do not possess a rigid political world view rarely vote in the primaries at all. The candidates who survive the primaries are necessarily more dogmatic, understanding that their politics must be well in line with the party platform. Whether by choice or by default, they constrain themselves from stepping out of bounds.

As a young State Representative in Oregon, I enjoyed the competitive spirit involved in winning elections and considering legislative issues. But I watched that spirit turn into belligerence when, during my second term in office, I gave birth to my first child just 10 days before the beginning of the 1981 Biennial Legislative Session. I hired a personal assistant from private funds, who doubled as a part-time secretary and nanny to help me with my newborn daughter, McKenzie. We created a small baby corner for her inside my office, knowing that during her first few weeks she would sleep most of the time. In between legislative hearings and votes on the House floor, I breast-fed McKenzie and we enjoyed a few moments of loving time

> Traditionalists are able to cooperate, as long as the cooperation unwaveringly supports the party line. Political issues are considered in black-and-white terms.

together in my office.

The Legislative Session is often characterized by a crazy schedule. Sometimes I would work late, but on other days McKenzie and I spent extra time together. This sort of flexibility worked for us throughout the six-month session. I felt deeply supported by the families who had let go of the traditional image of what a working family should look like. On the other side, I was severely criticized by citizens who believed I should choose between being a legislator and a mom.

> I was too young to fully understand the cultural war into which I had walked.

Dozens of letters to the editor of the local newspaper criticized me for taking McKenzie to the Capitol. The core message was that a traditional mother stays home to take care of the kids. If I wanted a baby, I should not have run for office. The controversy around my daughter set a new record for letters to the editor!

I was too young to fully understand the cultural war into which I had walked. I was doing what seemed natural and appropriate, given my equal dedication to public service and my family. To some, I was just doing whatever it took to balance all my duties as a mom and legislator. To others, I was a symbol of the breakdown of the family.

The media is fond of pointing out that members of Congress and U.S. Senators have never been more partisan, vitriolic, or mean-spirited toward one another than they are today. Political pundits report that they just don't like each other. It is difficult to find middle ground or even strike a balance of common courtesy in any political discussion, when our elected officials ascribe to diametrically opposed ideology. Political action committees (Traditionalist one-issue groups) can make a difference of one or two percentage points in an election, and therefore they wield significant influence in a close election. Most elected officials know this all too well. In order to win these deciding votes of a single-issue group, an elected official must go all or nothing: no compromises. Winning becomes an end in itself, even at the cost of one's dearest personal principles.

The American democratic system is built upon majority rule, which means, of course, that one side has to lose. This competitive form of government has left the public behind in crucial ways, fostering a great loss of decorum and mutual respect. Court appointments are now more overtly politically motivated than ever. Supreme Court judges, granted lifetime appointments so that they will be free to make impartial decisions, are now treated like political footballs. Their decisions and records are held in the closest scrutiny, and their nominations occasion the most vicious of party debates. Our courts have long been held as open to full debate, able to weigh all sides of an issue to increase the probability that fair decisions will be made on behalf of all people. Now, however, judges themselves are seen as political candidates. Once a judge establishes a record of upholding certain views, it is assumed she will maintain the same point of view indefinitely. The often-bitter conflicts between today's political party leaders allow little room for new ideas, perspectives, or possibilities that might pull us out of the boxing ring and into the light of collaborative solutions.

At this writing, our country is desperately divided, and the methods of Traditionalism will not help us out of the mess. Every political strategist knows that it is easier to defeat a candidate through negative accusations than it is to win an election through positive advertising. The politics of phobia, hate, single issues, dogmatic thinking, deception, and polarization will continue as long as Traditionalists in power continue to believe that the only way to advance their position is to promote fear.

Why Fear Sells

Stage Two Traditionalism employs the power of dread to motivate people, and today's modern media lends a hand. Breaking News flashing across our television screen informs us of fear-inducing events throughout the world. When an earthquake strikes China, when troops are attacked in Iraq, or when a strange disease hits Singapore, every detail is delivered to our homes in an instant. Wars are now viewed in real time and reporters are embedded with our troops. We are living in the first generation of instant world-wide news media. Those in charge of the Traditionalist power system have learned how to maximize fear and mobilize their forces against those who do not agree with them. Fear motivates us to defend ourselves, and therefore we continue to vote for the people who will protect us from our fears.

In *The Culture of Fear*, sociologist Barry Glassner presents a poignant example of this phenomenon, by focusing on the public's perception that crime is rampant. The level of our concern outweighs what the actual crime statistics warrant, he says, in part because of the media's frequent reporting of crime rather than good news. Local newscasts live by the dictum "If it bleeds, it leads"; thus drug, crime, and disaster stories comprise the greater portion of news broadcasts. Between 1990 and 1998, when the nation's murder rate declined by 20 percent, the number of murder stories on network newscasts increased by 600 percent. An astonishing statistic! This false fear keeps crime on the front pages so that law-and-order politicians can play a winning hand, and to guarantee healthy sales for local papers and high ratings for the nightly news.

In Stage Two of our political evolution, people are made into media icons and quickly become stereotypes, which are then used to evoke fear in the hearts of the public. To some political conservatives, Bill and Hillary Clinton are symbols of vice (and hence, of all that is wrong with our country). For liberals, the mention of Rush Limbaugh or George W. Bush evokes instant feelings of fear and revulsion—shades of an Armageddon that will rain down on America if such folks are allowed to govern or speak for the country. Stage Two Traditionalism makes use of a symbolic shorthand to vilify and demonize opponents, in hopes that the remaining party loyalists among the public will donate money, volunteer on campaigns, and most importantly, vote for their side—motivated not by their highest principles or their greatest hopes, but by their worst fears.

When I held public office, I occasionally observed legislators who would introduce legislative bills that had little chance of success, with some pretty twisted motives. Because the legislation posed a threat to a particular industry or interest group, the bill gave one or two of the legislator's lobbyist buddies the opportunity to pick up a new contract from the corresponding interest group, so that he or she could help defeat the legislation. In truth, the industry probably did not need the lobbyist in order to defeat the legislation, but being on the outside of the process, how would they know that? The industry could not afford to allow the legislation to pass, so they hired the lobbyist. A complex game played by insiders, Traditional Stage Two politics keeps most folks in the dark. The more such secrets are maintained, the greater our fear of what we don't know. And the greater our fear, the less likely we are to respond from our principles instead of reacting out of an instinct simply to survive.

Another common activity of Traditionalism is to assure that certain legislation does not pass—not necessarily because the legislation is bad but because it has been introduced by the "wrong" party. If one party resolves an issue so that citizens no longer experience the difficulty or fear associated with it, voters will tend to keep that party in power. The outcome of the next election is a constant concern for Traditionalism, under the auspices of which all legislative action or inaction depends on whether legislative votes will benefit them at the ballot box in the near future. The result of all this hedging and sidestepping is a breakdown at the legislative level. No longer bogged down by a mere preference for the status quo, Traditionalists are now faced with complete governmental stagnation. The lack of constructive action becomes the rallying cry for the next election cycle, each side blaming the other for how little has been accomplished. Deception is part and parcel of Stage Two Traditionalism. In this stage we feel stuck, with no one willing to shoulder the responsibility for solving problems.

The heart of Stage Two Traditionalist politics is the struggle for dominance. In Stage Two, success comes from overpowering one's opponent; each side of every conflict believes it is their duty to prove the other one wrong. The issues at the forefront of this cultural warfare are emotional and controversial: reproductive rights, gay rights, women's rights, civil rights, affirmative action, school prayer, and same-sex marriage. And of course, money plays a huge role in these arguments: whether the funds come from business regulation, political donations, or the tax structure. Like Stage One Anarchy, Traditionalism includes the firm belief that one's position is right and that the opposition is unequivocally wrong. The primary characteristic of Stage Two Traditionalism is not what one believes but that one believes it with certainty, leaving no room for the possibility that those who disagree might offer something of value to the public conversation. The primary political aim is to dominate, out of fear that the only alternative is to be dominated.

The foundation of fear and polarization that motivates Traditionalist politics is as destructive to our country as it is to individuals. When we are guided by our fears and by the desire to dominate others, we condemn ourselves to a powerless, reactionary state of being. We then shrink from our greatness both as citizens and as a country. Rather than being free to envision and create a system that reflects our inherent compassion and kindness, in Traditionalist politics we are reduced to a defensive position: pacing back and forth over the same territory again and again, going nowhere, just barely protecting what we think we have. In such a state, shared responsibility and respectful collaboration are out of the question, and solutions elude us. Our desire to protect ourselves becomes foremost in our minds. Like a wounded tiger that must kill in order to live, the Traditionalist stance holds us in attack mode—captive to our own fear.

The Two-Party System Gone Sour

Political Traditionalists are exceptional organizers, with a top-down hierarchy that empowers the leader to act and to rule. Control is extremely important in Traditionalist thinking. The Traditionalist acts according to firm boundaries and a set game plan; maverick notions are frowned upon. Thinking out of the box, creativity, is not welcome in the Stage Two political arena.

> When we are guided by our fears we condemn ourselves to a powerless, reactionary state of being. We then shrink from our greatness both as citizens and as a country.

Sadly, the majority rule that has governed our political system since its earliest inception has been corrupted by Traditionalist thinking into dominion over the opposing party. Partnerships forged on behalf of the collective good seldom thrive within its domain. The elemental concept of the "loyal opposition" that the founders once relied on to debate important issues has degraded into a hair-pulling floor tussle between the political parties.

I recently read that the first time President Richard Nixon mentioned his opponent's name was on election night, after it was certain that he had won. Notwithstanding the high jinks and skullduggery that went on behind closed doors, politicians 30 years ago employed rules of public conduct and decorum that have now been left behind. Addressing one's opponent by title rather than by name kept political debates less personal and more polite. When I served as a legislator in Oregon, we addressed one another as "the legislator from Salem" (or wherever) when referring to another representative on the House floor. As a freshman legislator, I was bemused and a little worried by this custom (not certain of my ability to memorize every member's hometown). Senior members of the House explained that this custom was a longstanding tradition from the early days in British Parliament, and was intended to maintain a level of civility. It was believed that members were less likely to get into heated debates if we refrained from calling each other by our given names. I'm not sure what happened to this custom, but I miss it.

The balance of power in Congress is now so sensitive that if a single member switches his registration to the opposing party, the entire leadership of the Senate is thrown to one side. The result is a blinding tension between the parties and their leadership, with the party in control lording over the agenda and the entire work of the legislative body. In Stage Two Traditionalist politics, manipulation and exploitation of others is the norm. The result: no one really wins.

I know many public leaders, especially legislative staff, who feel the limits of the two-party system. They want to work with staff from the other party yet feel the taboo associated with crossing political boundaries. Many staff members become sucked into the vitriolic behavior; like a herd animal that smells the first drawn blood, they must add their attacks in order to play the game.

A sad example of how I allowed myself to be drawn into this animalistic jungle occurred in 1990 when I managed a highly visible statewide race. Our candidate had just announced his candidacy for governor against the seating governor. We knew the race would be a hard-fought campaign. My friend announced his candidacy on a beautiful, sunny morning, flanked by his family and surrounded by hundreds of cheering supporters on the lawn of his childhood home. As campaign manager I wanted to capture in a phrase what I believed was one of the important strengths of our candidate: his strong family background and values. I turned to a reporter and said, "May the best family win." I was rather proud of myself at the moment, thinking I had spun a clever phrase.

> The winner-take-all climate created by the Traditional system means we treat one another with an enemy philosophy.

Sunday morning following the campaign announcement, the political reporter wrote a feature article about the newly-contested governor's race. The story described how the campaign manager had revealed the campaign strategy: we were going to run a family-centered race, pitting the governor's family against my candidate's family by using the phrase "may the best family win." I was horrified. That could not have been further from the truth. Never had there been a discussion inside our campaign committee of a family-versus-family political strategy.

I know myself to be an honest, kind person, and yet when I said those words I was unconscious of the harm I produced. This was a thoughtless phrase hurled against our opponent as if he were an object. Never would I purposely try to hurt another person or his family, or to pit one family against another. The winner-take-all climate created by the Traditionalist system means we treat one another with a philosophy of enmity. Candidates, election officials, their staff, and, often, the volunteers cannot avoid being pulled into the attack mode that is built into the system. I deeply regret the pain that phrase caused to both the sitting governor and my candidate.

Contributions of Traditionalism

Traditionalists are responsible, loyal and obedient people with a keen sense of right and wrong. Creating and maintaining rules that provide order is a fundamental tenet of Stage Two Traditionalism. In this way, hard-working Traditionalists bring stability to society by controlling destructive human impulses, though the end is usually accomplished by setting rigid boundaries. Historically, during times of transition and conflict, the Traditionalists' insistence on order has served our country well.

From the 1950s throughout most of the 1970s, Stage Two Traditionalism seemed to be fairly successful at managing the political affairs of our country. The two-party system dominated the general political discussion, and reasonable debates attempted to balance public perception of the issues at hand. At the close of World War II, the "good life" began, with an unprecedented number of Americans able to attend college on GI veterans' benefits, improve their financial future, and live in peace. The Republican and Democratic parties managed the affairs of the country, each in turn, according to the will of the voters. Our political structure generally elected men who readily accepted the traditional pattern of hierarchical leadership, and Americans followed in step. Political machines such as the Daly Chicago network were accepted, and the rules of the game were clear: those who wished to participate in politics knew what they had to do to climb the ladder of power. Most people belonged to one party or the other, and the idea of registering as an Independent was uncommon, even eccentric. Streets were clean, schools were well-managed, and families were happy. At least that was how it looked on television.

With the assassination of President John Kennedy in 1963, the escalation of the Civil Rights movement and the women's movement, and public protests against the war in Vietnam, our country experienced a sharp cultural division that persists today. The unraveling, the exposure of our hidden wounds and troubles, had begun. Problems of social injustice, racial inequality, domestic violence, alcoholism, drug addiction, and violent crime, problems of poorly educated students and a substandard health care system, began to come to light. The two-party system that Stage Two Traditionalism had contributed to American politics could not match the exponential speed of our social upheaval, nor could it illuminate the complex set of issues that the mammoth changes had evoked.

Prior to the cultural chasm created in the 1960s, Stage Two politicians had been able to run the country in relative obscurity, governing behind the scenes with little scrutiny by the media or public interest groups. Open meetings laws had yet to be passed, and deals could be made across party lines and in back rooms with the greatest of ease. Big money had not yet arrived in politics with full force, nor had 24-hour media pundits, poised to tell us what to believe. The public had been going about its business with very little awareness of the inner sanctum of the political system. The conventional perception was that good people were working hard to run the affairs of the country. Stage Two Traditional politics seemed to be working just fine.

While it is true that Traditionalist politics has made an indelible contribution to our American heritage, and that it successfully carried us from our revolutionary beginnings to our 21st-century position of wealth and prominence in the world, the petty polarities that have been a necessary evil of Stage Two are fast outliving their usefulness. Traditionalism, great as its past contributions have been, cannot give birth to the conscious public leaders who will successfully lead America through the next hundred years of global change.

Why Level Two Traditionalism Is Weakening America

If our nation's leaders do not move beyond Stage Two politics, they will be woefully unprepared for the demands of an interconnected and collaborative global society. Complex new social, economic, and environmental issues must be addressed, and sooner than we think. Traditionalism, with its fearful two-party polarization and backbiting, its simplistic black-and-white thinking is inadequate to meet these challenges. At this writing, both Democrats and Republicans are preparing for the next Presidential election, their common philosophy being survival of the shrillest. Who can denounce and dispatch the other first? Someone leaps from a corner of the ring and comes out swinging. What is the other to do? Defend himself, of course. Like all fights it is predictable, with each matching the other for power and punch. And what happens at the end of all this swinging and slinging of mud? The fighters emerge bruised and bloodied, more cynical and jaded than before. Even the spectators feel exhausted and a little dirtied by the whole display. This is the lamentable state of our American political system as it stands now, operating in a Stage Two Traditionalism that no longer answers the needs of the people.

> Stage Two Traditional politics has so thoroughly disillusioned a great majority of Americans that they have given up on our political system.

The "attack style" politics of the past two decades places all of us who participate into defense mode. The system proceeds in a circular path that repeats its mistakes and, in the bargain, excludes most Americans from the democratic process. Traditional politics has become so irrelevant to a growing majority of Americans, that it comes as little surprise that our best and brightest citizens are largely uninterested in political leadership. In its current form, Stage Two Traditionalism wastes our genius, drains our spirit, and encourages infighting. It's a system of values within which it is very difficult to reveal what is best in us. Politics based upon the idea that success is only possible through caustic debate and political dirty tricks cripples our country's vision and brilliance. As Deborah Tannen, in her book *The Argument Culture,* puts it:

> If you limit your view of a problem to choosing between two sides, you inevitably reject much that is true and you narrow your field of vision to the limits of those two sides, making it unlikely you'll pull back, widen your field of vision, and discover the paradigm shift that will permit truly new understanding.

Stage Two Traditional politics has not only limited our effectiveness as a nation, it has so thoroughly disillusioned a great majority of Americans that they have given up on our political system entirely. This rush to the sidelines, this desire on the part of so many Americans to drop out of the political system in the name of ethical self-preservation, constitutes the membership of Stage Three, the politics of resignation. If we examine closely the characteristics of this new and growing group of our nation's citizens, it becomes clear that reviving the dream of American democracy rests largely in their hands.

4

Silence and Resignation:
The Third Stage of Political Evolution

Life is always somewhere between retreat and renewal.

—Anne Morrow Lindbergh

This growing group of Americans, having retreated into resignation for a variety of reasons, secretly hopes to awaken from their withdrawal. For this reason, the Politically Resigned hold the key to evolving American democracy out of its current stagnation and into an era of hope.

The new Politically Resigned come from all walks of life. This growing cluster of Stage Three American citizens, a phenomenon that has only emerged in the last 30 years, now cuts across all demographics, including age, economics, and religious preferences. The Politically Resigned of Stage Three are so fed up with traditional American culture that we are creating an alternate set of values, unique consumption perspectives, and ecological ethics to answer our deep concerns about poverty and other social ills, as well as more global concerns about our government's conduct as a world citizen. These Americans are the same one-third who have withdrawn from participation in Stage Two Traditional politics.

I call this group *politically resigned* because they have acquiesced to the belief that American democracy is controlled by Stage Two Traditional politicians, and that they are unable to make their voice heard in today's political climate. They are resigned to the idea they cannot effect change in our current American democracy. The Stage Three Politically Resigned dwell in a state of depression similar to what Elisabeth Kubler-Ross describes in her seminal book *On Death and Dying*. Kubler-Ross was the first to observe that we all go through a similar process when faced with death. Her stages of death and dying have since been observed by many others as part and parcel of the human experience, not only of death, but of any form of loss. Kubler-Ross's original genius applies as well to the evolutionary stages of politics—Politically Resigned Americans are now experiencing a heartbreaking loss. They are watching the long-cherished American greatness fade into the shadows.

Political Depression and Withdrawal

The emotional state of depression is far more intense than ordinary sadness. I can attest to this from my psychiatric nursing background, as well as from my own emotional experiences. I am an optimist by nature, with high, spirited energy. From my perspective, the glass is almost always half full. During the times when I have experienced depression, however, I did not want to engage in life. I pulled the blinds and sank under my warm covers. The last thing I wanted was someone trying to cheer me up or tell me why I should feel better. My state of mind at such times was that of the Politically Resigned. No longer willing to face the day's challenges, we are pulling up the covers and sitting on the sidelines of American politics. Political resignation is not unlike depression. Rallying cries to "get involved" or "cheer up" largely fall on deaf ears.

In psychiatric terms, a depression is characterized by a physical change in body chemistry. The normal homeostatic equilibrium, both mental and physical, goes out of balance. Modern research has proven that our brain chemistry is altered during such depressed states. As a result, we do not respond to stimulation. In the most severe states of depression, we may become catatonic. The disorder labeled *catatonic schizophrenia* refers to a complete inability to speak or to move the body.

As a nursing student at the University of Missouri Medical Center, I cared for a young, pregnant girl in a catatonic state. I will never forget her acute unresponsiveness to any form of stimulus. She had been hospitalized in the third term of pregnancy because the doctors were concerned that she would not respond to labor pains and would not recognize when her baby was ready to be born. Since the girl did not speak and did not have a supportive family, her medical history was almost nonexistent. Because we could not determine her last menstrual period, her baby's due date was an educated guess. Her empty, straight-ahead stare, hour after hour, seemed to assert, "I am not here. I do not exist." We knew very little about the young girl's background or why she had, at such an early age, become so entirely withdrawn.

> Political resignation is not unlike depression. Rallying cries to "get involved" or "cheer up" largely fall on deaf ears.

Do we really understand why Stage Three citizens are depressed and withdrawn? Do we understand their current resignation toward American democracy? During what many believe to be one of the most exciting times in our country's history, why is it that so many educated and otherwise flourishing citizens are joining the socially marginalized and racially excluded, by choosing to withdraw from politics? The young, pregnant, catatonic woman may help us comprehend our current situation. It is quite possible that we are ready to give birth to a completely new form of American democracy, and yet we are stuck in withdrawal, numbed by our sadness and depression at the political atmosphere as it now exists. The harsh reality is just as it was for the pregnant woman who sat staring until the day her baby would be born. We will grow and birth this new being, this new democracy, because that is the natural law. All things change. The question is this: Will we engage in the evolution of our democracy consciously, cooperatively, with purpose and vision, or will we allow it to be formed and birthed in a fearful, reactive state? Will we simply sit and watch it all happening on TV, taking no action to help it grow into greatness?

Elisabeth Kubler-Ross observed that among her dying patients, those who faced their depression, sat with it and accepted the final stage of death, were able to receive and give love to family members who had drifted apart. In this stage of acceptance, she noted, dying patients spoke with more authenticity than at any other time in their lives. New life and relationship was created in the midst of death. How might we be similarly authentic in our approach to this "death," the small and large losses that accompany our current democracy? How might our courageous acceptance of these losses help us give birth to a new American democracy, one that our children deserve to inherit?

My Own Political Withdrawal

I had to face my own withdrawal from politics in the mid-1980s after I lost a statewide bid to become Oregon's Secretary of State. After winning my party's nomination in the spring primary election against two older, male candidates, I prepared myself for an intense statewide election against a well known, experienced candidate who had considerable name familiarity and backing. I worked hard, garnered a worthy level of support, volunteers, and enthusiasm, and raised our proposed budget. In the end I was defeated by a quality candidate who later became Oregon's first woman governor. By many accounts I lost the race because cultural conservatives from my party had decided I was too liberal. So, rather than support my candidacy, they nominated an independent candidate who professed more conservative principles. Post election-day analysis revealed that the independent candidate had probably drawn votes away from my political base, significantly hurting my changes of winning the election.

I remember the deep grief I experienced the morning after the election. I felt as if someone had surgically removed my heart, and that the cavernous hole which was left was vibrating with sorrow. A part of me had died. Losing is difficult, but losing in front of my friends and family while I watched the results being reported on the nightly news was the worst part. "Two weeks," I told my husband, "and I'll be back to normal." Little did I know that weeks, even months after the election, I would still be reeling as though I had just experienced the death of a loved one. A few weeks after the fall election, I saw one of my dedicated campaign volunteers approaching and headed for the other side of the street. I couldn't face answering what had now become an achingly familiar question: "What are you going to do *now*?" In my depression and disappointment, I did what seemed natural: I withdrew. I had to take time to reflect on what was important to me before I chose how I wanted to reengage in the political world.

Occasionally I would meet a campaign friend, and we would relive election "war stories," laugh, and have fun. I wrote thank you notes to the many friends and workers who had contributed long hours to the effort and reflected on how many wonderful people had become involved in the democratic process. A fundraiser was organized to help erase the campaign debt, and my gratitude grew for all those who had assisted and cared about me. Suddenly I realized that the campaign had never been about me: it was about honoring the democratic process and putting myself out there. It was about courage and vulnerability.

Gradually I began to heal. In the process, I was led to deeper questions about how we govern ourselves in this country. How could we discuss our differences in order to discover our grandest visions? How could we create a political system that attracted and nurtured all its citizens? What would attract leaders with higher motives, dedicated to serving the collective good? During my campaign for Oregon Secretary of State, I had met many leaders throughout the state. I valued the new access I had gained to statewide business, and to academic and community leaders during the year-long campaign. I sought their wise counsel. I had lost the election but I now had great new friends and mentors.

Suddenly I realized that the campaign had never been about me: it was about honoring the democratic process and putting myself out there. It was about courage and vulnerability.

About six months after the election, I asked 15 statewide community leaders to gather together to discuss these and similar questions. I wanted to hear their views and find out what could be done to foster authentic political leadership. Those who attended our meetings included the president of one of the state's largest technology companies, a financial services businessman, one of the partners in the advertising company that created Nike's early public relations success, a philanthropic visionary, a labor organizer, and a number of women leaders. We met three or four times, each discussion yielding rich ideas that affirmed our common dream of a fresh and genuinely open political conversation. I look back now and realize that these early meetings were manifestations of my burgeoning desire to see a new political culture taking shape. While specific action did not grow out of those discussions, I learned to act on my yearnings, those inner tugs of truth. The leaders who attended those early meetings nearly 20 years ago affirmed that I was not alone in my desire to witness the evolution of our country's democracy.

If the Stage Three Politically Resigned were to seek wise counsel now, revisiting our dreams of a new way of political life in the U.S., what inner riches might we discover? One thing is certain: if we as Stage Three citizens remain in a state of political depression, accepting a passive role in our country's evolving future, our disappointment will only grow deeper. My own story of awakening has been a long and bumpy one. I have learned that it is not always easy to transcend disillusionment and political withdrawal, and that disappointment often trudges side by side with us as we work to regain our hope.

In 1990, several years after my statewide campaign, I was asked to manage a highly visible and dynamic campaign for Governor of Oregon. A dear and talented friend, Oregon Attorney General David Frohnmayer, planned a run for our party's gubernatorial nomination. Dave was considered a strong candidate; early polls showed he had a good shot at unseating the incumbent. Since I had been on David's campaign advisory committee, I knew his philosophy and organization. We had worked well together through the years, so I gladly accepted the invitation to manage his campaign. I had had very little to do with politics since my own statewide race six years earlier and was excited to return to politics to work for such a worthy candidate: a Rhodes Scholar whose ethics were unequaled by anyone I had ever known. This was my return to politics. The depression, withdrawal, and disappointment had lifted. I was energized and rejuvenated, eager to work in support of a worthy candidate.

One February day in 1990, after Dave had announced his candidacy, raised considerable money, and enlisted hundreds of volunteers, the sitting Governor suddenly announced that he would *not* be running for reelection! His staff and fellow party leaders were just as shocked as we were. He had given no hint of retiring. The press corps came running to our office looking for Dave, whom they had declared the favorite to become Oregon's next governor.

The very next day, Secretary of State Barbara Roberts, who had defeated me six years earlier, announced her candidacy for governor! She had received good marks while in office and was one of Oregon's premier political leaders. Most observers believed Dave was the odds-on favorite to win. The newly-retiring governor had surprised everyone, so no one else in his party had prepared to embark on a statewide campaign. Barbara, on the other hand, had nothing to lose. The worst she could do would be to increase her political standing, were she to run a good campaign. What happened next took years for me to understand; it became one of my life's great lessons.

By the spring of 1990, the cultural conservatives in our party had expressed strong displeasure with Dave's pro-choice positions. They threatened to run a third party against him if he did not soften his views. This was déjà vu for me! How could this be happening? Here I was in yet *another* statewide campaign, my candidate and friend running against the *same candidate* who had defeated me six years earlier. And again I was faced with the threat of a third party candidate who could subtract important votes if Dave did not respond to criticism from our party's right wing. This was *Dave's* race for governor, but as his campaign manager I felt I was living a recurring nightmare.

The organization spearheading the third party candidacy asked to talk with Dave. I agreed to talk with them, as Dave was not available. I was incredulous at what they offered; it crossed every ethical political line I had been taught. The bottom line was this: they would agree not to run their third party candidate, provided that our campaign organization raised $100,000 for their political organization! In addition, when Dave became governor, they expected to review his court nominees, as well as directors of the government agencies dealing with child and family welfare issues. Until that moment I had never experienced even a hint of what could be called a bribe while in elected office. I called Dave and reported the group's request. He used many choice words in his response, telling me never to talk with them again and to get on with our campaign. I wholeheartedly agreed. We never spoke of the meeting again and had nothing more to do with them. But secretly, quietly, inwardly, a part of me had died.

That splinter group made good on their threat. They ran their independent candidate for the office of Oregon's governor and again siphoned voters from the conservative base. Dave lost the election. Fortunately for all Oregonians, Dave soon became President of the University of Oregon and has accomplished amazing achievements for the state in that capacity. I, on the other hand, retreated in disillusionment. One of the finest men in politics had just been tossed aside by his own party. In a classic example of Stage Two Traditionalist political thinking, the cultural conservatives who ran the third party candidate saw the issues in an all-or-nothing light, and insisted on their way. Many of the gentlemen I met with that day publicly espoused morality in politics, yet they had suggested political shenanigans that crossed every boundary of ethical behavior. The disparity sent me into a deep depression and a withdrawal from politics. . . again.

This retreat lasted for over 10 years, while I sorted through my views and passions for public service. What I had witnessed was shameful, yes, but no lives had been lost. No shots had been fired. Our democratic system worked. A candidate was elected and life marched on. But one question continued to haunt me. Will our political system continue to work as our technologically interconnected, global society becomes increasingly complex? Does our current democracy—rife with shrill voices, veiled threats, and tough talk—allow for a political conversation that serves the many and creates a worthy legacy for future generations?

Pondering these questions gradually renewed my spirit to recommit to the basic tenets of American independence and freedom, not as catch words but as my felt experience. I reengaged with new vigor and purpose. It was then that I became determined to write this book and, by doing so, to join a growing throng calling for the evolution of American democracy. What do you believe is the fate of our nation? What role are you willing to play? Do you dare to become a catalyst for the evolution of our freedom? What could you do, right now, to spark your reengagement?

Characteristics of the Politically Resigned

Whether leaning to the left or the right, with conservative or liberal views, the new Politically Resigned are a complex lot, not easily put into a box. Some polls claim this new group comprises almost 40 percent of American adults, or 50 million adult citizens. While I am not a researcher, political scientist, or sociologist, like many others, I have witnessed personally and sensed intuitively that a new political phenomenon exists in America today which has not yet been fully identified. I understand the plight of our "catatonic" citizens because I have been there, disgusted and choking in a toxic political atmosphere.

The Politically Resigned are extremely cautious. We feel frustrated at the ways mass media shrinks current events into sound bytes, at how politicians boil down complex global issues into pithy points that belie the deeper issues. While we are Politically Resigned, we view television and radio news as noise rather than substance, and we seek to control the information that enters our personal space. The Politically Resigned are discerning, even suspicious, of incoming political information, and continually examine the motives of those who sell the news. The Internet and other modern technology support our desire to become information truth detectives. We have access to world news stations that depict different views of America than do our internal media outlets. At anytime during the day, Internet news stories fly through cyberspace, espousing detailed and highly debated points of view. Magazines, editorials, and commentaries with diverse perspectives are available at the touch of a keyboard.

I recently heard an interview with a veteran news reporter who had spent six months covering the war in Iraq. He was returning to America after a two-week hiatus in London, where he had observed European attitudes and opinions of the war firsthand. This reporter stated that he had been covering the news since the 1960s, and that he was certain that citizens today are far more educated and knowledgeable about world events that at any other time in history. He marveled at the depth and breadth of the questions and insights he encountered. He felt that some citizens knew more about the war than he did, even though he had personally been working inside Iraq for six months. Amazed, he began to realize the vast wealth of news and information that is now available to people of average means.

Truth-seekers at every level, the Politically Resigned are acutely familiar with the impact of globalization on our culture, and we want to understand the whole picture. This politically silent group is painfully aware of the commonly quoted statistic that America comprises 4 percent of the world's population, yet consumes 24 percent of its resources. In *The Cultural Creatives*, Paul Ray and Sherry Ruth Anderson state that this group has "green" values and a concern for the ecology and well-being of the whole planet because we understand that our buying and consumption patterns impact not only our local communities but also the world at large. Deeply concerned about issues such as global warming and environmental destruction, we know that an honest conversation must begin among Americans so that we can embrace the kinds of lifestyle change necessary to head off global disaster. Most Stage Three

Politically Resigned citizens realize that our world is shrinking, and that to survive in a global society, we must live differently.

In my own case, my optimism resurfaced in response to a change of focus. I shifted from anger at what I considered to be the outer evidence of folly and began focusing my attention to what was going on within me. What were my highest values, my purpose for living? What did I want to leave behind for my children? Fueled by this new inner attention, my hope was restored.

Though we may still consider ourselves Politically Resigned, when we focus on areas of our lives in which we believe we can make a positive difference, our enthusiasm returns. This social activism rarely includes large organizations, however, and tends to exclude political parties, large unions, or associations.

It is simplistic to say that the Politically Resigned are an irritable bunch of liberals, because we're just as frustrated with the liberal Democratic machinery as we are with the right-wing Republican faction. This group is critical of almost all large institutions, from political parties to international corporate giants. Many of us were once gainfully employed with large urban corporations and dropped out of that lifestyle to pursue a quieter existence based on simple core values and a concern for the future of the planet. Some of us even aspire to live off the grid, erecting rustic homes in wilderness areas and disconnecting as much as possible from dependence on the prevailing infrastructure.

> The Politically Resigned are just as frustrated with the liberal Democratic machinery as they are with the right-wing Republican faction.

As long as we sit in Stage Three Political Resignation, we resent Americans who want to force their particular set of mores. We want to live according to our values and avoid the criticism of Stage Two Traditionalists. At Stage Three we deeply value personal freedom, but unlike Anarchists, who feel they must press their point violently, when we are Politically Resigned we rest in the knowledge that we are good and kind citizens who know what is best for ourselves and our families. It is a state of removed complacency. We do not need Traditional Stage Two politicians telling us how we should live. We feel that the government's role is to protect our privacy and freedoms, and then leave us alone. We feel justified in our separatism.

The Politically Resigned are confused about how the American founders' dream of independence and freedom has been altered over time. We may despair that the overwhelming majority of Americans has lost the desire for true personal freedom. Conversely, some of the Politically Resigned have given up on the media altogether, perceiving it as a biased and sensationalized corporate machine. This group shuns television newscasts and movies that seem to celebrate shallow, meaningless lives.

Despite our doubts, the Politically Resigned have not given up on American democracy. Quite the opposite, in fact. At Stage Three, we are highly appreciative of our freedoms and long to live in a democracy headed by ethical, noble, and conscious public leaders. Our very inactivity is an exercise of our freedom to choose: to decide how and when and whether to participate in self-government. Our burning question at this stage becomes, "How can I make a difference in my country without becoming drawn into systems and values that I abhor?"

Recent corporate scandals have further eroded morale among the Stage Three Politically Resigned. People with money and influence appear to control the American political agenda. Daily news accounts of $10,000-a-plate dinners that raise up to $10 million in one evening are mind-boggling to the Politically Resigned. We believe that while good people may successfully run for office, the system of power politics prevents them from accomplishing anything worthwhile even if they are elected. Newcomers to political office are quickly indoctrinated into the current two-party system that teaches incumbents how to run for reelection *against their opponents,* rather than by speaking and listening to the constituents. In short, in Stage Three of our political evolution, we are fed up. We have little or no desire to engage in the political discussion. One episode of a well known comic strip says it all. A cave man remarks to another, "Show me a man who will lie, slander, and swindle for one lousy vote," and the second adds, "And I will show you an incumbent."

Why the Stage Three Politically Resigned Will Never Become Stage Two Traditionalists

Evolution is by definition a process of growth, a gradually unfolding development occurring in stages. A series of complex changes takes place through abrupt modifications or mutations, and as a result of these changes, organisms learn and adapt. The evolutionary process is expansive, an endless surge of patterns constantly moving forward and outward—a kaleidoscope of co-creation.

In politics, as in any evolving system, what worked before does not work again in the future. As one stage of politics evolves, it gives rise to a new stage that surpasses it in sophistication and adaptive strength. At ever-greater levels of awareness, we adopt political realizations that include ever-greater numbers of humanity. The greatest among us aspire to fully inhabit Stage Four, the Politics of Hope.

> As one stage of politics evolves, it gives rise to a new stage that surpasses it in sophistication and adaptive strength.

Almost 50 years ago Abraham Maslow published *Toward a Psychology of Being,* sparking the human potential movement and widespread recognition of the innate goodness of human nature. He identified "hierarchy of needs" inherent in all human beings. As our basic needs security, shelter, food, and self-esteem are met, our opportunity for individual self-actualization grows. Unlike scientists before his time, who had concentrated their studies on dysfunction, Maslow took it upon himself to observe "well" people who were happy and productive. He discovered that people whose basic needs were met aspired to lives filled with meaning and purpose. In fact, he found that if people did not discover a life of community, purpose, and higher meaning, they became depressed and even violent. Human beings have an innate calling to become part of a community, a part of the whole, and to transform self-centeredness into a consciousness of the collective good. Scott Peck's *The Different Drum*, in turn, has outlined stages of community-building, explaining how the evolution of a community is based upon the self-actualization of its citizens.

While many Americans still struggle for minimum existence, the majority of our citizens live abundant lives. Affluent lifestyles, which politicians rightfully want to protect ("It's the economy, stupid!"), allow more and more Americans to move up Maslow's hierarchy into a greater awareness of the needs of others. Once we begin to move up the pyramid, there's no turning back. Martin Luther King Jr. spoke of this when he said, "I have been to the mountaintop." His inspiration lives today as one of the grandest examples of vision, a dream of a unified community of Americans living together in peace. The Politically Resigned among our Stage Three citizens are intimately familiar with, and daily strive to practice, humanity's noblest principles. As we emerge from political resignation, we will not fall backward down the pyramid to return to Stage Two Traditional thinking. The law of evolution and our natural desire to fulfill our greatest potential as human beings propels us forward.

Commitment Phobia

At the national level, the Politically Resigned—the entire group of Stage Three Americans, in fact—are fragmented and disorganized. This scattering phenomenon reveals a reticence to engage, not just in party politics, but in any body politic. At this stage, we have a kind of commitment phobia regarding all large organizations. This commitment phobia is a protective armor around our values. "We refuse to be sucked into an empty, hectic lifestyle not of our choosing," we say. The Politically Resigned find small and meaningful ways to belong—at the local and community level—that do not threaten our aspirations to live fulfilling lives.

The Politically Resigned have been burned. We have seen the great wall of denial characterized by scandals in politics, sports, entertainment, the Catholic Church, Enron, and Abu Ghraib prison in Iraq. We may organize neighborhood groups to build a new playground with ease, but traditional big-party politics leaves us cold. We have little or no interest in working for most candidates or party issues because it means adopting the party line. While we languish in Stage Three Resignation, the fact that we could alter the form and direction of American democracy does not occur to us because we feel so alone; we do not recognize ourselves as part of any group. We are a motley crew of ad hoc interests, reticent to call out to one another.

> What we all have in common in Stage Three is a nagging desire to make a difference.

What we all have in common in Stage Three of our political evolution is restlessness, a nagging desire to use our very real power and ability to make a difference. We don't make excuses at this stage; we simply choose not to participate. We sit on the sidelines because we believe that the mere act of participation would doom us to mischaracterization by some larger force; we want our individual values honored. Within the Politically

Resigned, energy, creativity, and vision are simmering, held in reserve, as though we are waiting for the right recipe to inspire the creation of an extraordinary meal we can as yet only dream about. Our pondering, our state of reflection, remains static, justified by our commitment phobia and vice versa. The dilemma of the Politically Resigned is not inescapable, but we must see it before we can take action to free ourselves.

Whether our political resignation comes in the form of a conservative desire to ensure that moral values are embedded in our society, or as the values of the maturing counterculture, our search for a more meaningful life persists. As Abraham Maslow pointed out, the purpose-driven life reflects our values and urges us to ask bigger, more personal questions. It is a search that begins with conscious inner reflection about what we are committed to, and which challenges us to make everyday decisions in full alignment with our highest principles.

The Politically Resigned are looking for a new way to live that has positive impact on the world. We do not want to commit precious time and resources, only to discover that we have become embroiled in yet another trail of meaningless activities. We fear being taken down a path of empty promises and disappointments. Like new lovers withholding our full commitment until true love is revealed, in Political Resignation we remain commitment-free, until we quite literally fall in love again with the purpose, power, and potential of American democracy. Our hope must be restored, our wounds addressed and accepted, the little deaths and big disillusionments grieved and passed through, so that we may again perceive a future beckoning for our vision. Only then are we ready to become engaged.

The Search for Authenticity

Stage Three citizens are not easily fooled; secretly, however, we long for the return to a mythical time when truth and honesty reigned supreme. We want it on a silver platter and on a global level. Something within us knows this is unrealistic, yet we have trouble shaking the great sadness that underlies our political resignation. One reason Stage Three citizens have become so disillusioned with politics is that modern political strategists and their candidates have made blatant use of technology to push their messages to special interest groups. An incumbent's message must now be highly specific in order to recapture votes. The resultant overload of radio, television, and direct mail sound bytes has overwhelmed us with self-centered, inauthentic communications from politicians. Most Americans have become sensitive to the superficial language that imbues political campaigns, but Stage Three citizens take it especially hard. In desperation and disgust, we protect ourselves by dropping out of the political arena altogether.

Joel Klein, campaign consultant for Al Gore in the 2000 presidential campaign, remarked in a May 19, 2003, *Time* magazine article on election politics, "There are reasons, mechanical and spiritual, why this sterile, straitened form of politics may have finally outlived its usefulness. People understand what shrink-wrapped language sounds like. They want to feel that politicians are speaking directly to them." When political leaders do not speak authentically, voters do not listen, and the result is that millions of people become resigned to a belief that their participation will not make a difference.

It is my experience that on reflection, most of us want the same things. Once our basic survival needs are met, we want to love and be loved, we want to express our creativity and contribute something of value. Above all, we yearn to live a life of meaning, to know that our time on this earth has made a difference. I believe that in order to rejuvenate our democracy and make it fit to address the challenge of our nation's world citizenship, the Politically Resigned citizens of Stage Three must awaken and reengage as compassionate, conscious activists. With so many gifts, what can't we create?

Stage Two Traditionalists have built the foundation of their political leadership on shifting sands, on issues that create division between people. More recently Traditionalists have invoked national security and threats of terrorism to motivate voters. In other cases, fear tactics are used to prevent cutbacks in government spending, to intimate that society as we know it will fall apart if budgets are balanced. Is it realistic to rely on the majority of Americans to continue to act out of fear and loathing in the name of American democracy? I think not. Fearful rhetoric strikes a hollow chord, especially in this time of increasing suspicion as to whether the media can be trusted to deliver the message.

Elisabeth Kubler-Ross's stages of death and dying suggest that we accept the wisdom of the dying process. I believe that as political beings, we must likewise accept the death of our current stage of American democracy: one built upon polarized parties, inauthentic power politics, favors for the few, mediocre actions based on short-term thinking, fearful attacks, and a pervading distrust.

By accepting the current form of our democracy as ineffective and outdated, we begin to accept its dying process not as a national disaster but as a natural part of the greater evolution of humanity. We can then begin to conceive of, and eventually give birth to, a fresh, new form of democracy. Exactly what this new democracy will look like is still a mystery. The question is, who will lead us? What values and visions will these new leaders possess? If the impossible were possible, if a new democracy were taking shape in America before our eyes at this very moment, would we not bring our most thoughtful, our most compassionate and best selves, to the political conversation? By accepting the death of the old system without rancor, we can revive our optimism and our will to carry our democracy to the next evolutionary stage. We become fully aware of what must be done. With open eyes and hearts in pain, we view the devastation before us, and our work as public leaders is suddenly all too clear. Before we pick up a single tool to rebuild, we cultivate the Politics of Hope. That very hope allows us to begin.

> By accepting the current form of our democracy as ineffective and outdated, we begin to accept its dying process as a natural part of the greater evolution of humanity.

My hope for the remaining Politically Resigned is that they become less embittered and more empowered, as was I, despite my deep disillusionment. My hope is that the would-be leaders among the Resigned rise out of political depression, and become catalysts to reawaken the greatness of American democracy.

5

The Politics of Hope:
The Fourth Stage of Political Evolution

I am not a visionary. I claim to be a practical idealist. I have not the shadow of a doubt that any man or woman can achieve what I have, if he or she would make the same effort and cultivate the same hope and faith.

—Mohandas K. Gandhi

Citizens in Stage Four of the evolution of politics know that all things are interdependent. We accept interdependence as a universal truth which we consciously apply in our individual lives—in all our actions and communications, in personal, spiritual and political expressions. Stage Four citizens have made the all-important shift from *me* to *us* consciousness. The concept is simple enough, but it is quite a challenge to apply it to political policy. It has reduced some of the bravest among the free to wither in confusion. Grasping the concept of interdependence, however, is essential to our human evolution; indeed, to our very survival.

One great leader who catalyzed historic change while simultaneously maintaining his honor and his hope was Mahatma Gandhi. A meek, shy lawyer inspired by his personal experience of the prevalent bigotry against Indians in colonial England, Gandhi understood the power of his people to work together for independence. Against all odds, Gandhi held out a central vision of change and united a people deeply divided by religion, economics, social strata, and regional politics. His nonviolent method was not only the means but also the core principle of his work. He did not vilify his opponents or speak in ways that created division. Gandhi knew the power of interdependence, unity, and collaboration, and he integrated these concepts in a way that empowered millions of Indians to obtain their freedom and reclaim their national identity.

As young children we gradually gain independence from parents, and we develop a sense of self while negotiating the tricks and traps of the big, wide world. As we grow we learn that we are not the center of the universe, that we must find ways to get along with family members, friends, teachers, and coaches. To become emotionally mature adults, we must fully integrate our awareness of interdependence with self-sufficiency, developing successful relationships in the worlds of work and social life. We arrive at this integrated understanding of our personal power and our interdependence by learning to listen to others, to respect the diversity of valid perspectives, and to receive new ideas with openness and optimism for the future. In this state we are not fearful of change. We welcome surprise and innovation, recognizing that while it is unfamiliar, the new and untried lights the path to greater human evolution and the promise of personal growth. We welcome new ideas with open arms and rolled-up sleeves, ready to change *ourselves* first for the sake of arriving at workable and ethical policies of self-governance.

Stage Four political leaders have fully integrated their democratic values and personal freedoms with an understanding of the interdependence of all. Such a leader looks at life in a larger context, aware that narcissistic views are in conflict with liberty and justice for all. Living from this greater context means evolving a spiritual understanding of one's relationship to mankind, the world, and the universe. No longer victims of black-or-white thinking, Stage Four citizens develop the ability to entertain and balance seemingly opposing concepts simultaneously. Our thinking is holistic rather than dualistic. Our view is global rather than merely personal. Due to the vast scope of our vision,

Stage Four citizens quite naturally inspire others, and just as naturally emerge as leaders.

The conflict between labor and management in business offers one fairly recent example of opposing views creating harmonious change by means of Stage Four leadership. Business owners long insisted that, were they to improve benefits and salaries or allow workers a voice in the company's management, profits would suffer. In a privately-owned company ("This is mine, not yours") the managers and owners felt they knew best. A few far-sighted business owners, however, had cultivated the ability to see beyond "us and them," beyond the context of the status quo. As a result, they drew a conclusion that many industry leaders now consider to be plain old common sense: workers closest to their customers or end users have the best information about how to improve products and service. These cutting-edge business leaders began to treat their workers differently: they listened, increased pay, and made changes based on employee recommendations. To the astonishment of the naysayers, workers felt an unprecedented pride and investment in their jobs, increasing productivity and decreasing turnover, all of which—rather than draining profits—saved the companies money. This model, unthinkable only 30 years ago, was rapidly adopted by mainstream American businesses after a few visionary CEOs perceived the whole, interdependent picture within their companies. All they had done was to understand that their profits were dependent on the goodwill and contribution of their workers. From the vantage point of the whole, *we* rather than *me*, these Stage Four thinkers deduced that sharing their wealth (increasing salaries and benefits) and connecting with their workers (involving

> With global interdependence as their primary context for any new endeavor, solution, or policy, Stage Four leaders envision trends and opportunities that others do not see.

them in company practices and procedures) would make everyone in the company richer! With global interdependence as their primary context for any new endeavor, solution, or policy, Stage Four leaders envision trends and opportunities that others do not see.

American pioneers who courageously traveled across the Rocky Mountains in covered wagons understood that it took many people working together to accomplish what at times seemed nearly impossible. They were tough folks who worked together to survive unrelenting challenges. This notion of cooperation for the collective good still smolders in the American heart, founded in our agrarian roots. For our ancestors, community barn-raisings, plowing the neighbor's fields, and even building entire towns together, one home at a time, were simply part of a way of life. In the culture of modern American politics, however, the concept of working together for the good of all is less common and only minimally understood.

Dan Brown's bestselling novel, *The DaVinci Code*, is a stirring story about the ancient search for the Holy Grail, the chalice used by Jesus of Nazareth at the Last Supper. In Brown's story, it turns out that the Holy Grail is a secret that holds the key to the power that keeps the Catholic Church in command. A select group of souls, all pledged to protect the whereabouts of the Holy Grail, have created a code (the DaVinci Code) to maintain its secrecy. The deadly mystery unfolds as, little by little, the code is cracked, and the object of the ancient hunt—the legendary Holy Grail—is revealed. Thus a transformative new era of human evolution begins.

What is the Holy Grail of politics? What secret, if revealed and applied, would evolve American democracy to a new stage of greatness? What mystery, if uncovered, could shift the actions and consciousness of our political leaders? I believe that there is such a Holy Grail of politics. Furthermore, I believe that once we know and put to use its secret, our minds and hearts are forever altered. This secret will, if we call upon it, give shape and form to our democracy's most honorable purposes and policies. It is not a political spin or a campaign gimmick. As old as Earth, it feels strangely familiar. Like all great secrets, it is deceptively simple, yet the living of it has the power to shift everything on a grand scale.

The secret of our return to hope is this: *All life is interconnected and all beings are interdependent.* Establishing interdependence as a foundational principle of American political culture means adopting new policies that reflect its wisdom. Government would then take a quantum leap. If the interconnectedness of all life were held as a self-evident truth in the same way that personal freedom is now fundamental to American thinking, it would alter the course of humankind and the future of our life on Earth. Legislators of opposing views would unchain themselves from robotic adherence to party structures and eagerly seek out new ideas to meet modern challenges. Legislators would place the highest value on working together to improve their policies and would pay less attention to defeating one another. Armed with this secret knowledge, the incontrovertible truth of our interdependence, political leaders would form creative alliances for the good of all citizens rather than for the comfort of a select few. The world would change, as it always has, and we would change along with it, in an organic process that would become as natural to us as breathing.

> If the interconnectedness of all life were held as a self-evident truth it would alter the course of our future.

A quote attributed to Chief Seattle speaks to becoming a conscious political leader:

> All things are connected like the blood which unites one family. Whatever befalls the Earth befalls the sons of the Earth. Man did not weave the web of life: he is merely a strand in it. Whatever he does to the strand, he does to himself.

A Grail Moment
Stage Four Politics in Action

Newly elected King County Councilwomen Julia Patterson and Kathy Lambert attended their first County Council budget meeting in December 2000. Both women had been elected to the County Council in the previous month and wanted to learn more about the budget issues facing the County before they took office in January. As both of them had recently served several terms as Washington State Representatives, they understood politics and knew what to expect. Julia, a Democrat, and Kathy, a Republican, came from different communities. It was said that the two fought like cats and dogs in the Washington State Legislature. During one legislative session, these women had such sharply opposing views that they requested a department head to help them mediate their differences on a bill. "Trust" was not an apt description of their relationship. Neither trusted the other's motives. What happened in that December budget meeting, however, changed their political relationship forever.

Kathy told me, "We watched the County Council members quarrel over small details. They took every opportunity to manipulate and to accuse each other of malicious intent. The back-stabbing, ugly things they said to each other were embarrassing. I could not believe my eyes and ears! I felt sad and deeply concerned. Then Julia reached over and put her arm around me and whispered, 'I will never treat you like that. No matter what happens, let's trust one another.'"

In that moment, Kathy and Julia made a pact that they would never intentionally harm each other. Each promised to trust what the other had to say and to assume that her actions and statements were truthful, in service of the good of all.

Now, even when the two County Councilwomen are too busy to

check in with each other in advance of a public Council meeting, they give each other the benefit of the doubt. Kathy reports another incident where their agreement came into play.

> Julia had worked on an important piece of legislation for four months. We had not had the opportunity to discuss one of the details before the meeting. When I raised questions in the public meeting, rather than believing that I was harming her work, she listened and responded by carrying over the legislation until my question could be answered. I could tell Julia was irritated, but she continued to give me the benefit of the doubt. After more research was done and some amendments had been made, she poked her head in my office door and said, "I am so proud of you for speaking up, even though you knew I wanted to complete the work and move the legislation forward." I said, "No, I am proud of you for trusting me even though I had not told you about my reservations beforehand. Anyone else would have questioned my motives and we would have ended up with an ordinance that was incomplete." Julia replied, "We really do have a better ordinance because of your change!"

What Julia and Kathy have learned is that by forgoing their tendency to argue on one side or the other, by combining their perspectives, they generate better ideas and, ultimately, better legislation. Kathy says, "We've built trust and synergy for our programs, even though we come at the issues from different points of view. Our pact to *genuinely listen to and trust one another* made the difference. We know now that our different perspectives make our work stronger, and we welcome input instead of rejecting the other's views."

It's a simple idea. We know that our marriages and family relationships do not thrive unless we are able to listen to each other and work together. How could such a simple concept have escaped the notice of our political leaders?

What happened in that moment when Kathy and Julia stood together in the Council Chamber? These two adversaries experienced a sudden shift in their point of view, a "Grail moment" that immediately propelled them into Stage Four political consciousness. That shift enabled them to move to a new stage of leadership, one that allowed for patient collaboration and trust.

What is it that enables us to see the world differently, all at once, such that we move up and out of denial, to live in the knowledge of our interdependence? What is the spark that quiets our individual egos, that calls us to work together for the collective good, that reshapes us into grateful collaborators rather than fearful combatants?

My hunch is that Julia's and Kathy's nonattachment to the County budget (they weren't yet active Council members) allowed them to see clearly the behavior of the current Council members and to declare on the spot that they wanted no part of it. In their previous experience serving in the Washington State Legislature, they had often been in conflict. In those cases, both women were deeply attached to the outcome of their individual work and ideas. Thus, when they ran into conflict each one protected her own work with the vehemence of one who is right. *You're either for me or against me.* Kathy and Julia had been staunch Stage Two Traditionalists.

As visitors observing the budget hearing process, Julia and Kathy witnessed a kind of political behavior so oppositional that they each immediately swore it off. In their own way, the two became resigned. They looked at Stage Two Traditionalism and felt pangs of depression about the political system that had elected them. It was Julia's and Kathy's brief yet thoroughly transforming moment in Stage Three political withdrawal.

According to the law of evolution, each stage must be experienced; the next stage is always born of its predecessor. Some mutation or imbalance takes place in nature, and a new species emerges as a result. In the arena of political leadership, passing through one stage to the next may take years or only moments. When we are open to learning and to the authentic communication that trust makes possible, we become capable of shifting our point of view in an instant, in order to serve the highest principles.

> According to the law of evolution, each stage must be experienced; the next stage is always born of its predecessor.

Our entire focus changes. Rather than constantly struggling to be the best, to stay on top, we work steadily to do our best, to maintain our honor.

From Stage Three to Stage Four: Resignation to Hope

Each of us remains in our current evolutionary political stage as long as we are still coping, adjusting, and attempting to bargain within our current mode of thinking. Once again, we can think of the stage of bargaining that Elisabeth Kubler-Ross observed in her work with dying patients. The dying often attempted to bargain with their God, with their doctor, or with anyone who would listen. Bargaining was a way to cope with the impending loss of life. "If only" is a phrase often heard from patients at this stage in the dying process.

In their life-changing budget hearing, Julia and Kathy had

observed the desperation that goes with intense political bargaining. When they saw themselves detached from the process and determined that they wanted nothing to do with this kind of political leadership, they moved swiftly through the third stage of politics and leaped to Stage Four: the Politics of Hope.

How long we spend at each stage of politics doesn't necessarily determine whether we will move to the next evolutionary stage. Rather, the depth of our personal learning determines how long it takes us to evolve. We all have moments of insight. An inner light goes on; some call it an *aha* experience. We suddenly "get" a new concept or spontaneously view a problem from a fresh perspective. In that moment we become new. We are no longer the same. We change, we evolve forever. We can never go back. If our individual learning occurs deeply and authentically in a vivid moment of recognition, we may move swiftly from one stage to the next, as Julia and Kathy did.

We have all that we need to make this leap. As members of a species that can think and make decisions, we are endowed with a miraculous power: the ability to become aware of our awareness. Our intellect and our neurological patterns allow, even support, our ability to know that we know. We do not have to experience pain, agony, and separation any longer than we choose to experience it. We have a choice! As individuals and as a new democracy, we can choose to evolve rapidly or we can choose to evolve slowly. Either way, *we will evolve*. The question is *how* do we want our cherished American democracy to move forward into the future?

In a flash, Julia and Kathy decided to move through their political depression. Their epiphany was instantaneous, and it has lasted because they made an authentic commitment to honor it, to put it into practice as active hope and trust. Two years later, in August 2003, Kathy and Julia decided to cosponsor the first-ever "De-publican" fundraising event, where they would jointly raise money to support their mutual reelection. Outrageous! To cosponsor a fundraising event with a member of the opposing party? The raised eyebrows of their respective party leaders did not deter them. Julia and Kathy happily report that finding friends in the opposite party now seems to have become a popular idea. The two women were recently asked to speak at the Governor's Prayer Breakfast attended by hundreds of state leaders. Many of Kathy's and Julia's old colleagues in the State House, those who had seen them engaged in so many political tussles, were stunned to see the two women leaders sharing the podium, espousing the virtues of collaboration.

Accepting Our Evolutionary Path

The Holy Grail of American politics is accepting the idea—and the reality—of the interdependence of all things, and then acting accordingly. Stage Four leaders have discovered the political Grail. They know how to create new political alliances without resorting to fear and attack. They welcome collaboration. They use power to inspire people rather than to dominate and control their political opponents. When we acknowledge and act on our interconnectedness in an effort to serve the public good, we enter a higher form of political leadership. This stage is similar to the final stage of the dying process. In her research, Kubler-Ross noted that some patients—those who accepted the idea of their death and evolved through the stages of denial, anger, bargaining, and depression—were given a new lease on life. By accepting the reality of their death, such patients were able to forge authentic relationships with family members, even despite years of fear, anger, and past judgment of each other. Eager to create meaningful exchanges in place of resentments, these people wanted to tell family and friends what mattered to them, to express their love and passions before they went. This new opening of communication from the dying gave their loved ones permission to heal and move on.

Conversely, when Kubler-Ross's patients did not accept their deaths, they and their families often experienced bitterness or a feeling that what really mattered was left unsaid. A close friend of mine who lost both his parents in the same year, said of his father's death that, even up until his last breath, his father talked about living to be 150 years old. He never acknowledged the obvious reality of his impending death, nor did he acknowledge the grief that some of his actions had caused others. This man's father had perpetrated severe physical, sexual, and emotional abuse. When my friend asked his aging father about this abuse that had occurred decades before, his father simply said, "I don't know. I don't talk about those things." The denial persisted. After his father's death, my friend's brother and sisters made it clear that they did not want a funeral service, saying, "We don't want closure." The lack of acceptance on all sides regarding their

> Stage Four leaders use power to inspire people rather than to dominate and control their political opponents.

shared pain left no room for healing. If they are not faced squarely, such wounds can be perpetuated for generations.

When we accept the natural stages of death and dying, we are healed and new life is born in us. The same is true for political expression and leadership. The good news is that the death of our limited thinking opens the way for new and greater ideas. Accepting what is dying allows a new age to be born. The founders of our democracy were Stage Four political leaders whose commitment to radical ideas and evolved concepts was applied at the perfect time and place. They gave their all for a new way of thinking and leading. These revolutionary Stage Four thinkers cherished their independence because it was hard-won, and forged a governing document of unprecedented optimism and interdependent scope. We can only imagine how dear democracy was to them, as we continue the political evolution of that democracy to answer the needs of a new and different world. In today's world, they might say, we must incorporate an ever-increasing need to emerge as a cooperative, "holistically democratic" nation, rather than a "narcissistically democratic" one.

It is time for Americans to accept the death of our total independence, putting aside naïve notions that our actions will not impact one another or the rest of the world. Either our national narcissism must die or we will severely stall our political evolution.

An Age of Interdependence

The political turning point at which we stand today closely mirrors the dilemma of the American founders. They loved their homeland, and yet they could no longer stomach the indignity of being controlled by its monarchies, both political and religious. The American founders were products of the Age of Enlightenment; they readily accepted the death of the established powers: kings and churches that wanted to rule their minds and deny their basic rights. The founders' correspondence is filled with their unanimous belief in humanity's highest potential.

In Thomas Jefferson's August 22, 1813, letter to John Adams he writes, "I very much suspect that if thinking men would have the courage to think for themselves, and to speak what they think, it would be found they do not differ in religious opinions as much as is supposed." And in John Adams's diary entry dated May 1, 1756, "If we consider a little of this, our globe, we find an endless variety of substances mutually connected with and dependent on each other."

These few dozen Colonial Americans were all greatly influenced by the emerging idea that people could and should think for themselves. In order to bring about the birth of a democracy, the founders had to *accept the death of tyranny as the governing force in their lives.* The shift also meant accepting the death of their role as victims and shouldering the responsibility for self-governance. To avoid a descent into Stage One Anarchy, the founders knew that they must create an alternative to tyranny—a new form of government that would protect the dignity of the individual. In a relatively short span, a few New England idealists were inspired to publish and bring to life their common vision: the natural law of the inalienable rights of all people.

> The political turning point at which we stand today closely mirrors the dilemma of the American founders.

Most forward-thinking people find themselves in a similar predicament today. Our circumstances call not for a physical revolution but rather for an evolution of the spirit that will elevate our democracy to that highest human potential that so inspired the American founders.

What happened during the Age of Enlightenment in America did not take the form of a unified mass movement or an uprising to set things right. The ideas that gave birth to our Constitution were voiced by a few visionaries who communicated often and supported one another as best they could. Although the way was often difficult, sometimes bringing them to fisticuffs, together the founders felt a new infusion of intellectual energy and conviction that the moment for change was *now.*

At the time that the Declaration of Independence was drafted, the idea of inalienable rights of all was not universally accepted by a majority of its citizens. Thus, many of those who signed their names to the Declaration of Independence were ostracized. A third lost their homes and all their worldly goods and another third were killed, had family members killed, or were imprisoned. The founders were detested and vilified by an angry majority. But ideas based upon universal truths, such as the basic responsibility of the individual to self-govern, have a powerful life of their own. If nurtured and brought to life by even a small group of inspired citizens, this dedicated inquiry into truth cannot fail to answer humanity's drive to grow and evolve. Such citizens readily perceive the need for change, as well as the people's desire to implement fresh solutions to old problems.

> The declaration of our *interdependence* will comprise the next phase of our political evolution.

Thomas Jefferson put the final pen to those thoughts and feelings, and did so eloquently. Jefferson brought the words, the moment, and the Revolution together as one. The founders declared their independence. Now, at this moment in American democracy, the declaration of our *interdependence* will comprise the next phase of our political evolution. Stage Three Politically Resigned citizens are poised at the edge of the Age of Interdependence, their speech and thoughts deeply engaged in secret hope for the uplifting of humanity. Sooner than we might expect, their actions will follow suit.

When a critical mass of conscious leaders realize that they are articulating and advocating a common vision of change, the recognition ignites a lightning response. Add to that our modern advantages in communication technology relative to Colonial America, and it isn't hard to imagine how quickly our democracy could evolve once the Law of Interdependence takes hold!

Already the soil has been prepared. The tragic attack on the United States on September 11, 2001, has drawn us into the global community. The Internet enables us to connect all corners of the globe in a nanosecond. We see images of human lives devastated by war, hunger, disease, and poverty, and we wish that no one suffered these conditions. It is as though we now witness the world and all its citizens firsthand, up close. Seeing their struggles and triumphs, we recognize our own.

The idea of our interdependence with all things is an ancient tenet of all the great world religions. It is the essence of the Christian Golden Rule, a concept that also infuses the writings of Hinduism, Buddhism, and Islam. Jewish literature expresses it this way: "What you hate, do not do to anyone." In Taoism, the interdependence of humanity is likewise evident: "Regard your neighbor's gain as your own gain, and your neighbor's loss as your own loss."

Moving from independence ("It's all about me") to interdependence ("It's all about us") constitutes a giant leap for many politicians. Yet it is the Grail secret of politics, and like all great truths, it will find expression. Interdependence is gathering velocity in the disciplines of science, religion, culture, business, and education. Political leadership may be the last sector to express the evolutionary shift that is already at play in the world at large.

Unfortunately, the current national conversation about political leadership is limited to discussing which party will win Congress and how that party will manage to remain in the majority. The "winner take all" political system that has served America for over 200 years is showing its flaws. It's a system based upon ideas born from another time in history. The futurist Eric Hoffer says it well when he states, "In times of change, learners inherit the earth while the learned find themselves beautifully equipped to deal with a world that no longer exists." Our current political leaders are the "learned" within a system they would prefer to perpetuate, even though that system has become largely irrelevant to the needs of the evolving global community. We all sense that something is drastically wrong. The awakening of another group of learners, those who understand the interdependence of all, is essential if our democracy is to grow into a realistic player in a world of shared power. Our process of political evolution begins one person, one leader, one choice at a time.

Applying the Law of Interdependence

While it is not always easy to apply the Law of Interdependence to political policy, Stage Four activists strive faithfully to do just that. You do not have to be a Mahatma Gandhi or a Martin Luther King to understand and apply these qualities. Each individual citizen chooses thoughts and actions that serve to accelerate their personal evolutionary process. The effect is a cumulative power that grows into political movements that spark real change. In his book *Living Buddha, Living Christ,* the revered Buddhist teacher Thich Nath Hanh says that the next era of leadership will come from the collective actions taken by many individuals rather than from a single human being. I believe that each one of us must join the collective action for good, taking steps to see that our vision of democracy is not only preserved but also evolves to meet the needs of an interdependent world.

As we have seen, King County Councilwomen Kathy Lambert and Julia Patterson are political leaders who have transformed their political service and who now lead from a Stage Four point of view. Their contribution has begun a groundswell of bipartisan activity, and who knows how wide-reaching the effects of these two leaders' efforts may become? In time, such actions have the power to change the course of human events.

Even as they spoke of and fought for their independence, the founders of our democratic system understood the power of cooperation and *inter*dependence. In his famous essay *Common*

Sense, Thomas Paine wrote, "The cause of America is in a great measure the cause of all mankind." The founders' intention was to fight on behalf of *all* human beings, based on the idea that each individual had a divine right to think and act according to his own volition. Once it was accepted that preserving individual freedom was paramount among the responsibilities of a democratic government, regular debates ensued regarding the application of this radical new concept. Thomas Jefferson, John Adams, Benjamin Franklin, Thomas Paine, and many others engaged in intense and eloquent formal arguments about how best to apply the principle of individual freedom. These debates ranged in theme from states' rights vs. federal rights, to the extent of the power of the presidency, to the proper role of the military, to the issue of taxation. Today we are still debating these issues, and the United States Supreme Court often weighs in on the more thorny points of law. The founders' early debates continue to give credence and substance to the decisions made within every branch of our government.

Were we to enjoin a debate to consider the means to balance our independence (the freedoms inherent in our personal and national identities) on the one hand, and our global interdependence on the other, we would be propelled forward into our future. Much as our nation's founders were, we would find ourselves plunged into difficult debate, with an ever greater need for deeply considered reforms. It wouldn't be easy. It wouldn't always look noble or admirable to onlookers. But a debate of this nature, a conversation designed to discover what is best for generations to come, would exact from us the collective accountability that we expect of people in any true democracy. We could then look back at this time in United States history knowing that we considered our future and the world's future together as one, and that we acted with wisdom. The application of these two apparently opposing concepts—independence and interdependence—requires not only intelligence and open communication but also a heartfelt commitment to collaborative inspiration. To revive our democracy, we must be willing to peer into the distant future, to grasp the magnitude of political forms as yet unknown and untried, and we must have the courage to try them.

The Paradox of the Holy Grail

For a moment, imagine balancing these two ideas as though they were physical objects. In your left hand, you hold the idea, "We hold these truths to be self-evident. That all people are created equal...." Feel its power and weight, its substance. Now in your right hand, imagine holding the idea, "All life is connected and all human beings are interdependent." Sense the enormity of this idea. Feel its weight as well as the mystery and challenge it holds for the world of public policy. Now imagine bringing your hands together and joining the two concepts. The fusion of these two powerful ideas means the end of "the right hand not knowing what the left is doing." You are holding a holistic vision of democracy!

Each part of democracy, our interdependence as well as our independence, gives form and shape to the other, the way a riverbank lends form and shape to a river. In the same way, without containment by the concept of interdependence, our fierce desire to protect our independence will, like a rising river, overflow and flood the surrounding terrain, washing away precious topsoil, eroding the fertile ground in which we could have grown our nation's greatness. Unchecked and unbounded, even our precious independence will lose its value, picking up toxins and waste as it gradually consumes all that stands in its way. The same force of independent freedom, however, banked by interdependence, creates a viable habitat for the lives that flow within it and carries in its current the promise of a healthy future. By balancing our individual freedoms with a global consideration for the collective good, our democracy—like a clean, clear river—can sustain and nourish us, reflecting the light of our highest principles.

Applying these principles is no simple task. Evolving our public policy by adopting a global consciousness of democracy may be the toughest hurdle yet for our relatively young nation. We will not know the nature of the challenge, however, until we begin it—not until our individual conversations, relationships and actions make the shift in focus from *me* to *we*. That conversation must begin with the understanding that as United States citizens and inheritors of the most powerful nation in the world's history, we must come forward and take courageous steps in the evolutionary unfolding of the human spirit.

Serving *We* Before *Me*

When citizens and leaders shift from a *me* to a *we* context in considering public policy, there is a complementary adjustment in our assumptions about how and to whom we offer service in our lives. We move from a short-term view of concern for the problems of our immediate lifetime to a long-term perspective that seeks to serve future generations long after we are no longer around to enjoy the fruits of our labors. When an individual's egoic needs no longer dictate her actions, she is free to serve from an expanded perspective. Such a person easily perceives the whole of a matter, rather than having to divide it into small compartments. Her decisions become simple and direct rather than complex and tortured. This fundamental principle is just as true of a nation as it is of a single person. Making this shift from *me* to *we* becomes the firm ground beneath us, the foundation of a true democracy, that supports our steps as we work to meet the challenges of an increasingly busy and chaotic world.

Martin Luther King, Jr. knew well that he was marching and speaking on behalf of future generations, and he did so at his own peril. He treasured his four small children and wanted them "to be judged not by the color of their skin but by the content of their character." He held the same dream for his grandchildren, and for their children and grandchildren. King's strength of vision and persuasive power, however, did not arise from self-concern or even from a concern for his family. He moved from the *me* concern of the mere survivalist into the *we* perspective that wished a fair future for all people, all children.

In coaching sessions with my political leadership clients, this shift in perspective constitutes an ongoing struggle. My clients are kind, highly principled people. There's no question that they want to "do good." Without exception, they run for public office based on a strong desire to serve selflessly. It doesn't seem to matter whether they are "business conservatives" or "social liberals." Their desire—their need, in fact—to serve is what calls them to participate in democracy. It takes considerable inquiry and persistent reflection to unearth the assumptions that lurk underneath that desire to serve. I have found that becoming aware of these assumptions reveals our true motives for seeking public office. When my clients get fearlessly honest with themselves, they begin to see how much the ego's needs are entangled in their political plans. When an egoic need rather than spiritual purpose has moved them to run for office, political candidates become confused about how they will serve the public good, at which point a heartfelt sorting-out of priorities ensues. The same process occurs even for those of us who don't intend to run for office but who seek to serve as responsible citizens, conscious of the good fortune we enjoy by living in a democracy. When our egoic needs drive us to place *me* before *we*, our vision becomes distorted, our motives become confused, and it is difficult to truly serve the collective good.

Part Two of this book lists Seven Essential Practices that can guide you to make conscious political choices, whether at the level of public office or as an individual citizen. One of these practices deals with uncovering your true motives, so that you are free to serve with purpose and passion. A clue to understanding a citizen's or a political leader's true motives is revealed by asking about their legacy. When serving based on egoic needs, a person will often speak of the legacy *she* wants to leave after *her* death: *me* rather than *we*. A hope-filled Stage Four political leader, however, acts with *we* in mind, and aspires to a legacy that will benefit many generations to come. Her actions and decisions in the moment are consciously weighed and chosen based on the level of that benefit; her vision of a legacy overrides her immediate ego needs and desires.

> When an egoic need rather than spiritual purpose has moved them to run for office, political candidates become confused about how they will serve the public good, at which point a heartfelt sorting-out of priorities ensues.

The Shift from Fear to Hope

Stage Four political leaders are moved to action by hope, trust, inspiration, and vision. We understand the inevitability of the evolutionary process. We know well that humanity, despite its apparent outward chaos, is busily evolving into a cooperative species. The primary challenge in Stage Four lies in maintaining this perspective. Stage Four citizens have faith in the inherent goodness of all things and work to stay mindful of actions that might thwart us from continuing to evolve into nobler, kinder beings. Whether the leap forward takes place within the animal kingdom or the human community, Stage Four leaders believe that the evolutionary process will take place and that it is intended to take us all to greater heights. The Stage Four point of view is founded in faith; it has its roots in a spiritual sense of responsibility toward all of life.

This certainty, this trust in the evolutionary process, forms the foundation of the Stage Four citizen's hope. When we know that a thing is sure to unfold, we are less attached to the specifics, and this viewpoint allows us to relax, knowing that the whole is already complete and perfect. No matter how much or how little of the picture we can presently see, we know that in time all will be done. Armed with this hope, Stage Four leaders have the courage to say, "Come and follow me. I know where we're headed." This is the quality that gave so many the courage to follow the examples of Mahatma Gandhi and Martin Luther King. They had a clear vision of the mountaintop and thus were able to inspire others to climb the mountain along with them. They allowed their highest intentions to serve humanity to fuel their actions instead of becoming caught in the current state of things, which bogs down so many otherwise great thinkers and activists. These great ones prevented themselves from being washed away in the sea of appearances by building their platforms on higher ground. Doing it for *me* is never enough to keep us going. But doing it for *we,* for all of us, is always worth whatever it takes.

Stage Four political leaders do two things extremely well: they are aware of their unique gifts, and they use their personal power and vision to share those unique gifts with the world. They cause their gifts to become a powerful force for good. Many citizens are aware of their unique personal gifts yet choose to keep their abilities hidden from public view. My personal coach once told me, "It doesn't matter much if you are a great artist, if you keep your paintings under your bed." Stage Four leaders have decided to bring their paintings out from under their beds and share that beauty with others. This is one of the primary distinctions that separates Stage Four from Stage Three citizens; Stage Three has chosen to withdraw from the public view and serve their highest principles, but only within the confines of their immediate family and community.

There's nothing wrong with focusing on family and community, of course. However, when millions of Americans choose not to actively participate in the political system, the result is a lesser vision and an anemic national dialogue. What if Thomas Jefferson had kept his genius under his bed? In what rudimentary stage of evolution might America still be languishing if Abraham Lincoln had not chosen to continue to run for office despite suffering defeat again and again?

By moving from fear into a vision of hope based upon faith in our evolving human nature, ordinary citizens become Stage Four political leaders. Such citizens understand that the same evolutionary principles which apply to all species and cultures also apply to our political culture. We recognize that this is a pivotal time in world history, that we exercise the ability to choose our destiny on a daily basis, and that to be conscious

> The Stage Four point of view has its roots in a spiritual sense of responsibility toward all of life.

of our dreams and desires is to *call them into being*. In Stage Four of our political evolution, hope motivates us to work *with* others rather than settle for power *over* others.

Collaboration: Power *With* Rather than Power *Over*

Business leadership models that have made their way into the mainstream in the past two decades have much to teach us about how to use power, not only in the workplace but also in American politics. Since the early 1980s, research conducted at Harvard, MIT, Stanford, and Notre Dame, among others, has demonstrated the importance of collaboration and has explored practical applications for people working together in teams rather than working against each other in fierce competition. In study after study, workers were asked what they considered to be the greatest qualities in a leader, and highest on the lists were the "soft" qualities: respect, integrity, fairness, and honesty. The tyrant who yells, belittles, and dominates others is no longer our vision of a great corporate leader. When workers feel inspired and are respected as individuals, when they observe corporate leaders doing what they say and saying what they do, a transformation takes place inside an organization. Because they believe that their role is valued and essential, the workers bond with the purpose and values of their company and pull together to give their best efforts. In such situations business leaders have seen, in action, the collaborative concept of power *with* others as opposed to power *over* them.

Today's political leaders are caught in a bind. Most of the American public, still engaged in Stage Two Traditional thinking, want a political leader who is a hero: one who will solve all the country's problems and make them feel safe. This notion became even more compelling in the wake of September 11th.

As I have mentioned, the new leadership style that works best in our corporate organizations, our families, and our communities is a collaborative and inclusive, open-minded model. But when our elected leaders do not appear strong and dominating, when they refuse to crush the opposition, they are roundly criticized. They are often reviled for being weak or soft on issues of security or crime. How is it that we have so compartmentalized our political culture that we apply different rules to politicians than we apply to other kinds of leaders, or to ourselves?

How does a person who wants to participate in elected political service bridge this gap between stages of leadership? Stage Four leaders understand that wherever we stand, a transformative shift is taking place in all areas of our lives. They know that although the world of political leadership may be one of the last arenas to respond to cultural change, respond it will, in due time. Our hope and faith in the evolutionary process allows us not only to accept but also to welcome the gigantic global shift that is destined to transform both American democracy and our nation's relationship with the rest of the world. For this reason, Stage Four citizens lead the change rather than wait for the change. Whether citizens or public officeholders, we are leaders first and foremost. Instead of merely wishing for change to manifest, instead of merely complaining that change is long in coming, Stage Four public leaders, those actively practicing the Politics of Hope, choose to work with others to bring about positive change. We take conscious action to cooperate with the evolutionary process, thereby accelerating humanity's journey to greatness.

Spiritual Activism

Stage Four leaders have learned how to live with uncertainty while continuing to move forward with faith. This is the delicate balance of spiritual activism. It doesn't require detailed plans but rather a general attitude of trust that the information and guidance needed to help us negotiate unfamiliar terrain will emerge and become clear as we ourselves evolve. Spiritual activism means assuming leadership and service out of a sense of gratitude for, and a felt responsibility to share, the gifts we have been given. Thus, we are moved to take action to improve life for others who will come after us. We take such action based on divine inspiration, accepting that whatever outcome has its origins in a pure and selfless motivation will, in time, find its natural perfection.

One of my favorite readings from Unity's *Daily Word* refers to hope as the "confident anticipation of blessings." The contentment that arises from faith in the goodness of humankind grants us the confidence to anticipate blessings in the future. This confidence forms the basis of our spiritual activism.

Did the founders of our government have a clear picture of this new idea, a democracy? No, they didn't. The uncertainty of the future did not deter them, however. Their focus was not on fear of the difficulties that lay ahead. Instead, confident that they would receive divine help, the founders sought inspiration and allowed themselves to be guided. Although the steps they would take were still hidden in shadow, they felt a sense of urgency that left them no choice but to leap into the unknown.

> Spiritual activism means assuming leadership and service out of a sense of gratitude for, and a felt responsibility to share, the gifts we have been given.

Stage Four leaders enjoy the unfolding mystery of our evolving political interdependence. Such citizens are at work in the world in ways that give meaning to our lives. Acting thus in alignment with our life's purpose propels us to spiritual activism, which, far from exhausting us, fuels our energy. Due to our trust in the evolutionary process, Stage Four leaders reveal a natural patience with outer political events that might appear to short-circuit our path to higher consciousness. Some take our equanimity for naiveté, when in fact it is evidence of a larger perspective.

Historians have described five crossroad points in our history: the American Revolution, the Civil War, the two World Wars, and the Cold War. Future historians will quite likely describe our present time as a sixth significant crossing point for American democracy. Will we accept our destiny, our inherent responsibility as a country of wealth and privilege, using our power to lead the world in sharing the earth's resources? Are we willing to do the work to exemplify a new, more inclusive kind of freedom? Or will we languish in a narcissistic independence and fail to model our spiritual diversity and greatness? I believe that when a critical mass of citizens embrace their spiritual activism, a transformational leap is bound to occur.

Beyond Liberalism and Conservatism

Our words and labels continue to divide us. When potential clients call to ask about political leadership coaching, they often ask, "Are you liberal or conservative?" Politicians are so used to being asked this question that it has become a convenient shorthand for defining themselves and others. Political consultants repeatedly say to them, "You must label yourself socially moderate and fiscally conservative." However, as we make our evolutionary crossing, as we learn to balance our independence with our interdependence, these words cease to have meaning.

Liberal often means an expansive role of government, in which the federal government may take the lead on a number of issues. *Conservative* usually means a restricted role for government and state, a deference to local government as the service provider whenever possible. In the social and cultural context, the word *liberal* may refer to someone who tolerates less government interference in the individual lives of its citizens, while a social *conservative* may refer to someone who believes in a stronger role for government to ensure that certain moral values are enforced. Fiscally speaking, *liberal* may refer to a greater role on the part of government, which means more money will be spent and taxes may go up. A fiscal *conservative* envisions a more minor role on the part of government, and therefore less spending and lower taxes. Stage Four public leaders know that none of these labels—labels that keep us separate from one another, preventing any real in-depth communication—work any longer, and they know that such stereotypes are a detriment to creating collaborative alliances for the good of all.

At this dynamic period in our country's history, many of us are experiencing a state of consciousness similar to the catatonia suffered by the pregnant teenager I observed as a student nurse. Remember? She sat and stared, unresponsive. Americans, too, have become unresponsive to old ways of talking and thinking that simply no longer make sense. We sit and watch, speechless and somewhat numb. But there is an alternative.

Imagine that young teenager coming alive, participating in the birth, and smiling as she sees her newborn child. What joy I would have felt witnessing a conscious, participatory birth rather than the grim forceps delivery that actually occurred. As a nation, we have a choice. We may continue to fall into the catatonia of labeling, limiting language, and narcissistic thinking. Or we can consciously choose to become a transformative world power that brings others along with us into a new state of freedom, a new kind of independence. I believe in the Politics of Hope. The laws of evolution are unfolding and our country is evolving into a new way of being in response to the pressures of a changing world. This birth will occur whether we want it to or not. The question is this: Will we be catatonic or conscious when it happens?

6
From Resignation to Hope

Hope is not the conviction that something will turn out well, but the certainty that something makes sense regardless of how it turns out.

—Vaclav Havel
Former President of Czechoslovakia

Whenever I present the outline of the Four Stages of Political Evolution to my clients and seminar participants, the concept has a potent impact. Viewing the process of political evolution leads them to new insights, because there is power in naming our political philosophies in relationship to others. For the Stage Three Politically Resigned, considering political leadership within the context of the Four Evolutionary Stages helps to explain our complex emotions regarding the current American democratic system. Learning how many millions of Americans share the same deep concern for the character of our nation's political process helps us feel a lot less isolated.

For most of our country's history, Americans have been taught we are either Democrats or Republicans. We are either liberal or conservative. The idea that our human political leadership philosophies *must* advance, through evolutionary growth cycles similar to those of all living organisms, is a refreshingly hopeful notion.

Remember the story of Seattle's King County Councilwomen Julia Patterson and Kathy Lambert, who broke through their partisan bickering and discovered the power of collaboration across party lines? They took the risk to act differently on their political convictions, viewing their relationship as Council members as far broader than simply liberal or conservative. They decided to relate to each other as two people doing their best to live their highest principles. To do so, they had to become willing to cross old political boundaries and to bear the wrath of state and county party leaders. In just a few moments during the budget hearings they attended, Kathy and Julia had a revelation: they saw what it was going to look like if they, too, fell into the same old partisan, personal squabbles. They both knew, for the first time, that doing their political business the old way would be much worse than creating a new alternative, no matter how much criticism they attracted in the process.

> I have discovered that, in discussing the Four Stages of Political Evolution, people begin to find where they fit within the spectrum.

In short, the two leaders felt they had no choice. Taking a leap into the invisible was therefore actually easier, not really a risk at all, given the fate that would befall them should they stick to the partisan norm. Though Julia and Kathy had been elected within a Stage Two Traditional structure, they chose to evolve into Stage Four thinking and to transcend the limits of the political labels they had worn. The result for both women has been an upsurge of powerful inspiration, an even greater concern for the collective good, better legislation, and a saner working environment.

In my work as a political leadership coach helping prospective candidates throughout the United States, I have discovered that, while discussing the Four Stages of Political Evolution, people begin to find where they fit within the spectrum. They evaluate the list of qualities and review the assumptions underlying their behaviors. Surveying the breadth of our ever-expanding human awareness (whether we view it through the lens of Elisabeth Kubler-Ross's stages of death and dying, Erik Erickson's stages of human development, Scott Peck's stages of community, or Don Beck's Spiral Dynamics of human consciousness) helps us choose how we want to grow and progress. As we move from one evolutionary level to the next, bringing with us the learning of the previous level, our newly increased awareness gives us more and greater insight into what we want to become. We expand into our nobility by paying attention to what matters most to us and by striving to model our lives after people we admire. We grow by looking more closely at our innate gifts and by thinking deeply about the practical ways in which we might share those gifts with the world.

The Candidate's Wife, My Greatest Teacher

My career in Stage Two Traditional elections gave me an opportunity to review how I was serving the public. After I lost my statewide bid for Oregon's Secretary of State, I took time to reflect on my gifts and the contribution I wanted to make. The loss sent me into a personal withdrawal: Stage Three Resignation. I questioned my motives and my abilities. What did I really have to offer? I was depressed. Assuming that I didn't have what it took to be a politician, I decided to go into business. I worked long hours learning to manage people, money, and products. I opened several successful food stores, served as the national franchise chairperson, and threw myself into learning a new career. I decided that political service was not among my talents.

After five years, our Attorney General and my personal friend Dave Frohnmayer called to discuss his potential bid for governor. He wanted to know if I would consider assisting the campaign. Secretly I had wanted to renew my belief in the political system all along. I said yes. With newfound excitement, I reengaged in the political process. Now that I was a successful business owner, managing a campaign seemed well within my abilities. Armed with both political and business experience, I felt ready for the tough world of politics again. But things had changed in my absence. After Dave's statewide announcement of his campaign for governor, the leading newspaper's political reporter called me and said, "So now that you are the spin doctor for Dave's campaign, how are you going to spin yesterday's announcement?" On that gorgeous fall day in 1989, I had never even heard the term *spin doctor*! During my six years of Stage Three Resignation and withdrawal from politics, the language of campaigning had completely changed. What we had formerly referred to as plain old *manipulation* now had a fancy new name that made it sound like a legitimate professional specialty: *spin doctor!*

After we lost Dave Frohnmayer's campaign for Oregon's Governor, I questioned the entire partisan election process. Somehow I had allowed myself to be sucked into playing a role I had never wanted to play. But how could I have avoided it? I wasn't aware of an alternative. My dilemma became especially acute during the tense last few days of the campaign. One of Dave's polls showed that the independent candidate (sponsored by a religious fundamentalist group) was eroding the number of our conservative voters, based upon the abortion issue. The only way we envisioned winning the three-way race now was by drawing moderate voters away from the other major party candidate. Our political advertising consultants wrote several hard-hitting advertisements to accomplish just that. We had been pretty aggressive with our message already, running a TV advertisement with visuals of shattered glass that demonstrated what would happen to our state if our opponent was elected. The image and the language of the ad was stark, dramatic, and highly critical. The committee and I approved it, but we later fired one of our consultants over the issue of using negative ads. At this point, however, in the last few days of the campaign, we were anxious for a win. We got ready to embark on yet another round of negative ads, this time to be aired on the radio.

One morning I was on a conference call with our radio consultant, the campaign's general political strategist, and Dave's wife. We had to know within minutes whether we were going to make the final radio buy. Dave was not available for a couple of hours, so we asked his wife to help with the final decision. It was the kind of frantic moment in a campaign when a quick decision can mean the difference between winning and losing. We had no time to waste.

We listened to the radio advertisement, briefly discussing the content and why the negative claim of the ad was such an important issue on which to attack our opponent. It was professionally scripted using an actor's voice. The ad was polished and ready to go—all we needed was final approval. Dave's wife listened to it once and then a second time. After a long pause, she said, "I would rather lose this campaign than run negative ads like that. I will not jeopardize my husband's good name and character by running those ads." We were stunned. The consultants and I tried to talk her out of her decision. We felt the situation was desperate and that we would surely lose if we didn't move in to destroy our opponent's moderate political base. We had been attacked from the right; we had no choice but to return the attack! Couldn't she see that? Only the candidate's wife stood in the way of us doing our job at all costs, winning the campaign for Dave. To her, however, the choice was crystal clear: Dave's character, his positive regard among the public, and living in alignment with their values was far more

> "I would rather lose this campaign than run negative ads like that. I will not jeopardize my husband's good name and character by running those ads." We were stunned.

important than winning the election or our approval. She wanted Dave to win, too—but not at any cost.

I learned one of my life's most valuable lessons in that moment. Dave's wife showed me the power of never forgetting your values and who you are, even in the heat of battle. I had forgotten that. In my eagerness, I had become focused only on doing a "good job," which, since I was the campaign manager, seemed clearly to mean winning the election. As a Level Two Traditionalist, I only saw how it might help our campaign in the short run if we succeeded in making our opponent look bad. I had lost sight of how it could hurt us in the long run if our candidate's values were shattered in the process. Dave did lose the campaign, and soon afterwards he brought his political expertise to the role of President of the University of Oregon. His Stage Four collaborative style has brought many new successes to the university. He has taken the University of Oregon to new heights of academic success, increasing fundraising as well as by creating a winning sports legacy. The university continues to grow and thrive under his leadership. Such is the inevitable outcome for anyone who understands his core values and insists on leading others only if he can do so in alignment with those values.

So what happens to candidates who are willing to do whatever it takes to win, even when it means crossing ethical boundaries? When they win, unfortunately, they conclude that any action justifies the end result, and thus they may continue to push their ethical boundaries to the limit. Even the most well-meaning candidates learn from consultants that negative, divisive advertising wins elections. Indeed, that was the only option our political consultants had offered us during the Frohnmayer campaign. We *had* to attack, they insisted, in order to marginalize our mainstream opponent. The candidates and politicians who survive such mudslinging battles end up mouthing clichés: "Politics is a dirty game. You'd better get used to it." Or, "Winning is everything because you can't get anything done unless your team is in charge." Or worse yet, "Don't get mad, get even." Such woeful incantations help justify the winning candidate's activities, however unscrupulous, as "all part of the political game."

This tit-for-tat Stage Two thinking has dominated American democracy for many decades. But the urgency and scope of today's global issues demands that our political leaders stand on higher ground. The sadness I felt about my own behavior during Dave Frohnmayer's campaign sent me into a bout of political resignation that lasted over 10 years. I vowed to have nothing to do with politics ever again. I retreated to the background, working on local school elections or community parks and recreation programs, rather than be sullied again in the big, bad world of politics. I did follow the political news, but only from what I considered a safe distance. It was a dark time for me. I knew that if someone like me, who so deeply believed in the greatness of democracy, had given up on our American political system, then many other citizens had surely done the same. I noticed that derisive jokes about politicians became more and more prevalent. Gradually I stopped even acknowledging that I had once served in the legislature, and I certainly didn't want to admit that I had managed a governor's race. When asked about my political past I downplayed it, saying, "Oh, that was so long ago; it was like another lifetime." I felt a gnawing regret that our American political system seemed to be drowning in a sea of negative assumptions and paranoid points of view that could apparently defeat even people who had the best intentions.

Through the next 10 years of resignation and withdrawal, I continued to have internal conversations with myself. I kept

> The urgency and scope of today's global issues demands that our political leaders stand on higher ground.

thinking about what Winston Churchill had said about Americans: "They always do the right thing.... It may be after they have exhausted all other alternatives, but they eventually do the right thing." How would we, as a nation, eventually clean up our political warfare so as not to exclude the thousands of good people who wanted to serve the public? How would we ever be convinced to reenter the fray? Day after day I wondered what it would take for me to entertain the idea of running for office again, despite the prevailing critical atmosphere. Each time I asked myself these questions, I found new and deeper answers. And little by little, to my amazement, I began to notice that something vaguely familiar was stirring within me: *hope.*

The Sisters of Hope

Following the governor's race, I had the good fortune of being introduced to the Sisters of the Holy Names of Jesus and Mary, and I later assisted their community with a large retirement project they wanted to build on their land. This beautiful piece of property was only a mile from my suburban home, and I was already familiar with their plight. The Sisters needed a land use permit to proceed, but the neighborhood had objected, not only putting a halt to the construction of their retirement center but also costing their spiritual community hundreds of thousands of dollars that they didn't have. The new retirement center would allow them to stay on the land they had settled almost 100 years ago, and would help them care for their aging population. I felt that all the Sisters needed in order to garner the necessary support was to tell their story, but I soon learned that their modest lifestyle had not prepared them to create a public conversation about their needs. I thought I might be able to help, so I volunteered to serve on an advisory board for a couple of years. My decision to lend some free advice turned into a nine-year relationship for which I will always be grateful.

It was from the Sisters that I learned the essential qualities of living within my values, speaking up for what I believe, and living well within a community system. Their loving yet tough nature taught me that it was possible to disagree without being disagreeable. I became convinced that leaders, in political life and elsewhere, can and must serve based upon a higher collective good, and that divine guidance can be found within all things. I was reminded that our individual gifts are not ours but are intended for the good of all. For this reason I began to see that during those times when I was afraid of risk or censure, my silence had served no one. I learned from the Sisters that the most gratifying joy in life comes from sharing our gifts.

> I learned from the Sisters that the most gratifying joy in life comes from sharing our gifts.

The Sisters were not stingy with their love and appreciation for my political work on their behalf, which accomplished full legal approval of their project. In fact, not one person testified against the Sisters' second application. The lovely retirement center was built, and the retired Sisters, as well as several hundred residents from the surrounding community, now enjoy retirement living in the competent hands of this spiritual community. Working so closely with the Sisters of the Holy Names and witnessing their nurturing ways in times of agreement and disagreement revived my spirit. Once again I understood the importance of acting on my passion for public service.

My life took several turns during the next few years, including a divorce after almost 30 years of marriage, moving from my home state, and putting down roots in a beautiful new community. All these changes allowed me to ask myself, at this crossroads of my middle years, "What do I really love? What are my unique gifts and how might I share those gifts with the world?" Fortunately, I had the time and resources to research work opportunities and to assess my strengths and passions. What I discovered was a wonderful integration of my several loves, bringing together politics, leadership, writing, and speaking. It all came together in the emerging profession of coaching. The underlying principles of personal coaching are founded in the human potential movement, which holds that each person is innately good and wants to live a meaningful life based upon offering her passions and gifts. The principals were deceptively simply on the surface, but I soon saw they were a great challenge to apply, especially for people who chose elected public service. I also found, to my dismay, that very few of my professional colleagues wanted anything to do with politics.

At my first professional coaching association meeting, at which over 75 coaches were present, I attended a round table discussion about learning to coach different kinds of professionals. One participant asked the panel members about coaching politicians. Someone piped up, "Why would *anyone* want to coach *politicians*?" After the laughter died down, I felt chagrined and disappointed. This was exactly the group that I wanted to coach. But I would not be dissuaded.

I have now experienced firsthand the power of personal coaching for my clients. I have seen how their political candidacy is transformed as they discover their highest motives in running for office and their true purpose in serving the public. As they detach from their accustomed fear of losing the election, they begin to speak with greater authenticity and a contagious enthusiasm. I believe that the inner work so integral to the coaching process encourages my clients not only to become better political leaders but also to be more effective *people*. I look forward to the day when

I hear that the President of the United States has called upon a personal coach, rather than a pollster, to help determine the presidential message and plan of action.

As a professional coach, I challenge candidates for public office, as well as elected officials, to understand their roles in reviving the dream of democracy. The work answers my aspiration to help restore the nobility of American politics. The journey from Traditional Stage Two politics through resignation and withdrawal, and into renewal, through practicing the Politics of Hope, is no less than life changing. It is an odyssey that every American citizen owes it to himself or herself to make.

The chaotic and ever-changing global society in which we now live demands that we understand the workings of this evolving organism we call democracy better than ever before. It means that each of us must assess our passions and gifts, and ask, "What do I want to contribute to the collective good before I leave this Earth?" As beneficiaries of a democracy, American citizens are blessed with abundant resources and unprecedented personal freedoms. As such, our political role at this unique time in history is to evolve and revive the dream of democracy so that it may find its greatest expression. We must become the nation we dream ourselves to be: one which, in every point of practice, reflects the balance of our collective interdependence with all things. Without citizens committed to living it, the dream will remain a dream. It cannot become real without your vision and participation. Whether you run for office or consciously choose some other political path unique to your heart, the time is now. The task is urgent, and it begins within you.

Part II

Seven Practices for Becoming
a Conscious Public Leader

7

Finding Your Spiritual Center

Spirituality cannot be something a person toys with, a little compartment of their lives. It has to be at the core, in a way that affects every other part of their lives.

—Steven Covey

The visible work of public servants is directed outward into the physical world. Conscious public leaders, however, know that the work of the external world begins first inside the human heart. Matthew Fox expresses it this way: "Work comes from the inside out: work is an expression of our soul, our inner being. It is unique to the individual; it is creative. Work is an expression of the spirit at work through us." The unique work of a conscious public leader is an offering of the self and the spirit.

Spirituality is essential to conscious public leadership. In fact, to anyone who says that spirituality has no place in politics, I would say that spiritual awareness has always been at the heart of the political process. The question is: what is the quality and character of our political spirit? Is it a spirit of win-lose, of fearing others and making them wrong? Or is it a spirit of collaboration, of hope and faith in others, and of a desire to inspire?

The impulse to recognize and to live in full awareness of the spiritual spark ablaze within us is the sustaining force behind all the world's ancient religions. We speak of the soul in Christianity, the Buddha nature in Buddhism, *neshamah* in Judaism, the *atman* in Hinduism, *nafs* in Islam. Whatever it is called, fanning that spiritual spark within us, recognizing it in ourselves and others, is the highest goal and the lasting purpose of human life. *How* we achieve this lasting experience of the divine is what separates one religion from another. Ironically, our attachment to these differences has caused thousands of years of war, as well as the annihilation of countless world cultures. Overcoming our tendency to divide ourselves remains our greatest *political* challenge.

The essence of our spirituality is apparent in the biblical statement of Jesus, "The Kingdom of Heaven is within you," and in Mohammad's words, "Those who know themselves know their Lord," as well as in the Hebrew Torah: "He is in all, and all is in Him." The Tao Te Ching states, "In the depths of the soul, one sees the Divine, the One." The interconnectedness of all things is clearly an ancient and universal idea, and it has yet to become part of our *political* consciousness in America.

In presenting the Seven Essential Practices for becoming a conscious public leader, I am drawing a distinction between religion and spirituality. What religion, if any, you choose to incorporate into your life is a decision that includes culture, family background, and a multitude of personal values. Spirituality, however, is a state of being which does not necessarily include adherence to any particular religious institution or philosophy. Dr. Roger Walsh, in his book *Essential Spirituality*, defines *spirituality* as "the direct experience of the sacred." It is this experience of the sacred—sought through introspection, prayer, meditation, yoga, contemplative walks, reading, or journaling, hiking through the wilderness, or other means—that brings us into awareness of the spiritual spark within all. By consciously engaging in such practices on a regular basis, we are able to move out of our customary mental whirlwind and gain access to our spiritual heart, where we may glimpse the sacred, where we find out what it means to feel blissfully aware.

Religion, on the other hand, implies a group of people bound together by shared beliefs expressed through specific symbols, icons, or rituals. When our beliefs prevent us from accepting another's path to the divine, we find ourselves disconnected, unable to experience the oneness and beauty of all things. Indeed, most of the world's wars have been fought over conflicting religious beliefs. The human journey to spiritual awareness has many avenues, and no matter how various our paths may be, our conscious actions can unite us. Our spiritual life does not have to include fearful separation or a self-imposed ignorance of differing views. A conscious public leader understands his own spiritual path (even if it is uniquely his). At the same time, he respects the spiritual understandings of those he serves, and with whom he serves.

> By consciously engaging in such practices on a regular basis, we gain access to our spiritual heart, where we find out what it means to feel blissfully aware.

Many in the business leadership community understand this concept of spiritual unity in diversity and are already making use of it in the workplace. Bob Shapiro, Chairman and CEO of Monsanto, said, "I am one fellow along with you. We are both going to die. We have a common destiny. We're in this together." The more we accept our common fate and our common spirituality, the more we are empowered to lead consciously in the political arena. In *Leading with Soul*, Lee Bolman and Terrence Deal write that the heart of leadership begins in the soul and spirit of each person. Being a great leader in the business world, or in politics, doesn't mean giving up spirit and soul.

The Politics of Hope, built on an awareness of the interconnectedness of all things, incorporates the essence of all great religious teachings. The challenge for conscious public leaders is, above all, to understand deeply and completely one's own personal spiritual values and philosophy, to ensure that our actions flow from our inner convictions. Accepting this challenge, we commit to a lifetime of steadily unfolding inquiry that ultimately makes us kinder, stronger, more inclusive, and more intelligent human beings.

The brilliant modern-day philosopher Ken Wilber distills the essential messages of the major religions into seven main tenets: (1) Spirit exists. (2) Spirit is found within. (3) Most of us don't realize the spirit within and live in a fallen or illusory state. (4) There is a way out, or path out, of this fallen state. (5) If we follow this path to its conclusion the result is a Rebirth of Enlightenment, and a direct experience of Spirit within. (6) This marks the end of suffering. (7) And social action of mercy and compassion on behalf of all beings begins.

It is the seventh tenet—the vision of social action of mercy and compassion on behalf of yourself and all beings—that I am challenging you to attain. Here we begin moving into a mode of collaboration. All that we do as public leaders from this point on, we do for everyone and not just for ourselves. From this evolutionary stance of hope we come to listen and work together in ways that carry universal benefit to all.

The Politics of Hope assumes that we each have ready access to the spirit within. When our awareness of our own spirituality is born, we join the ancient sages in seeing that essence in others. Herein lies the challenge: whenever we allow the outer world's appearances to override our inner reality—of goodness, of greatness—we will revert to a fearful view of ourselves as separate from one another and small. Before we know it, we have once again split the world into the good guys and the bad guys, and we stand ready to divide and conquer.

What Is Your Spiritual Orientation?

Of course, there is real danger in this world, and it is our duty to protect ourselves and others from harm. In order to navigate our course successfully between legitimate risk and the power of faith, as conscious public leaders we must ask ourselves: Do I see the world through the lens of fear or through the lens of hope? How you answer this question will direct a great deal of your policy decisions.

There was a young man who lived his life in such fear that he refused to leave his house. When asked why he was so afraid, he said, "A tree might fall on me, or lightning might strike me." We think this way when we see the world through the lens of fear. Yes, there is a remote possibility of being struck and killed by lightning. Sometimes we are so filled with foreboding that living indoors in total isolation can seem the only safe option. However, this man saw all of humanity and nature as his potential enemies. While this example may sound like a ridiculous extreme, it is not far from the foundational point of view shared by public leaders operating in the Traditionalist politics of fear and polarization.

> Do I see the world through the lens of fear or through the lens of hope? How you answer this question will direct a great deal of your policy decisions.

Throughout history, the great spiritual paths have taught that human beings can recognize the divine spark that exists within all. When we feel and experience our spirituality, we easily perceive it in others. Remembering our spiritual nature, we become capable of conscious public leadership. We gain a greater perspective from which to begin transforming our nation's political policies for the highest good of all. It is an altogether new way of winning, without losers. This is what it looks like to live in the Politics of Hope.

When we embrace our own spirituality, we begin to perceive the spiritual spark in other beings also. And behold—the pressure is off! Suddenly we have room for compassion, and love flows into our simplest daily actions. When this happens, we exchange the drudgery of having to defeat those who are "wrong." We begin to honor others, we listen differently, we even laugh out loud at the same human experiences we all share.

Spirituality doesn't mean pretending that everything's okay, when obviously a lot has gone awry. Quite the contrary! Sharing our spirituality means that we have more work to do than ever. It means that we become conscious of our own gifts as never before, and that we feel a kind of spiritual urgency to share those gifts. At the same time, we practice seeking, acknowledging, and evoking the greatness in others wherever we find it, and this in turn expands our capacity to collaborate and to inspire each other. Understanding our essential spirituality makes living on earth together feel purposeful, and often joyful.

> Sharing our spirituality means that we become conscious of our own gifts as never before, and that we feel a kind of spiritual urgency to share those gifts.

If we have harbored notions of ourselves and others that kept us feeling separate and small, the perception of our spirituality pulls the rug out from under this old thinking. We are forced to ask ourselves, "Why am I here at this time? What matters most to me? What are my gifts and how might I contribute?" Our view of ourselves becomes clearer. We spend less time pounding on our shortcomings and more time contemplating the multitude of possible forms into which our personal gifts may flow.

When we begin to deeply consider how best we might serve for the benefit of all, we encounter a grim surprise. We bump up against our fears and inadequacies, our secret belief that we aren't cut out for greatness. As we take on our work as conscious public leaders, we must begin at the beginning: with ourselves. Once we have addressed our own spiritual longings and the depth of our own suffering, we can begin to lead with compassion. Any work that we do is then infused with this sense of purpose, and there is no end to the good that may come of our efforts. In *Return to Love,* author and minister Marianne Williamson speaks to the powerful import of accepting our inherent greatness, rather than shrinking in fear from our imagined shortcomings:

> Our deepest fear is not that we are inadequate. Our deepest fear is that we are powerful beyond measure. It is our light, not our darkness, that most frightens us. We ask ourselves, "Who am I to be brilliant, gorgeous, talented, and fabulous?" Actually, who are you not to be? You are a child of God. Your playing small does not serve the world. There is nothing enlightened about shrinking so that other people won't feel insecure around us. We were born to manifest the glory of God that is in us. It's not just within some of us; it's in everyone. When we let our own light shine, we unconsciously give to other people permission to do the same. As we are liberated from our own fear, our presence automatically liberates others.

As we are liberated from our own fear, our presence automatically liberates others. This is a powerful and poetic description of the shift that occurs when we become open to our spiritual core. *Your playing small does not serve the world.* That's like the gifted artist whose paintings are all hidden under the bed! So many of us have eclipsed our gifts and in turn we have become unable to see the gifts in others. *It's not just within some of us; it's in everyone.* In this way, we are all inextricably connected to one another. Becoming reacquainted with, really contemplating, our spiritual selves brings us into a higher plane of thought altogether. No longer satisfied with grasping, we seek to give. We begin to think, speak, and act on the basis of higher motives.

Questions to Ponder

These are questions to contemplate, to help you look more deeply into your personal convictions. There is no right or wrong answer. Your answers may evolve and unfold over time as you begin to incorporate a clearer sense of your great inner worth. Answering these questions can help you begin to find your place in the Politics of Hope.

1. Describe your God (or whatever term you use to describe the Creative Source or Higher Power). Be as specific as possible. Include images, feelings, emotions. Include any words that help you go deeper into this question.

2. Think back upon your personal experiences of the sacred. How have these experiences altered your view of what is needed in the world today?

3. How you describe your God is often a description of yourself. What did you notice in your description of God that is also a description of yourself?

4. Look over your description of God. Is this the view of God that you want to continue to hold?

5. You may not believe in any form of God. If not, what do you believe? How does that belief affect your philosophy on public leadership?

6. Think of a time when you had deep feelings about an issue affecting your community, your home state, or the nation as a whole. Taking a bird's eye view of the issue, where was God, or spirituality, in relation to that issue for you?

8
Serving with Higher Motives

We live by what we get. We make a life by what we give.

—Winston Churchill

Like all leaders, conscious public leaders use our personal and political power to make things happen. The difference lies in our motives. Rather than following a desire to accrue personal wealth or fame, conscious public leaders are guided by higher motives. While there's nothing inherently wrong with the American dream of having the comfort and ease that money brings, when such desire becomes the primary motivating force in our lives, it doesn't take long before all of our actions are proceeding from a place of greed. At this point, it's no wonder that our political effectiveness, not to mention our global reputation, is greatly compromised.

Committing to practice the Politics of Hope means embarking on a process in which we grow into higher motives. With greater and greater awareness of our motives, we begin to act increasingly from an inner commitment to spiritual excellence. We serve principles before persons. As a result, we gain self-respect as well as the respect of our peers. We are then naturally empowered, by virtue of our virtues, and are able to use our power (personal, political, or otherwise) to serve others. This concept of service first and self second which forms the basis of the world's great religious philosophies, is the central goal of the Politics of Hope.

Using Personal and
Political Power for Higher Motives

Public leaders have power simply due to their position of authority. An elected politician who holds a committee chair or party position wields a great deal of power indeed. So what is power, then? My general definition of power is this: Being able to get the results that you seek by speaking your wishes and making them known. The magnitude of your power can be measured by (1) how fast you get your desired result, and (2) the degree, the depth and breadth, to which your desires are realized. All public leaders have desires for particular results. The conscious public leader's desires, however, are based in the higher motives of service. She seeks particular results not for herself, but for the good of all.

A committee chairperson has the power to determine which proposed legislation will be introduced and which legislation receives a hearing, work session, or vote. The chairperson reserves the option to postpone the meeting or to adjourn at a moment's notice if she does not like the nature of the deliberation taking place. A committee chair possesses a wide scope and depth of power to get her desired results in any given meeting. When the committee chair makes her desires known, they are immediately fulfilled. Thus, her actions directly affect the agenda and the outcome of the meeting.

A single committee member, on the other hand, may request that legislation be heard, but if the chairperson doesn't want to hold the hearing, it simply won't happen. The committee member's depth and breadth of power is limited in comparison to that of the chairperson. However, an individual committee member wields significantly more power than an ordinary citizen who stands in the hallway hoping to follow the testimony and count the committee votes.

One becomes a conscious public leader by exercising personal and political power in alignment with higher motives, a state of being that follows naturally from remaining open to divine inspiration. When the force of one's personal power is combined with a desire to serve without personal reward, one's political vision is infused with new inspiration. It is in this state of being that leaders rediscover the joy of public service and reap the personal satisfaction of contributing positively to the lives of others. As we consciously press our gifts into service with our hearts in the right place, our lives unfold effortlessly and are filled with meaning.

As we have seen, Dr. Abraham Maslow expressed the difference between lower motives and higher motives in his model of the Hierarchy of Needs. By studying healthy, highly functional people, Maslow discovered that all human beings need security, shelter, food, and water. Once these basic necessities of life are met, we grow into higher levels of life expression through our work and in our communities, eventually reaching the optimal state of being that Maslow dubbed self-actualization. When we focus obsessively on satisfying materialistic desires, we live on the lower rungs of existence, unable to move into the higher levels of human expression. In this state, the virtues we so desperately need and which are central to practicing the Politics of Hope—patience, generosity, creative cooperation—elude us. By practicing nonattachment from personal gain, we begin to live within these higher levels of being. As conscious public leaders, we express true compassion. We become able to genuinely love, honor, and serve the common good without desire for reward.

> As conscious public leaders, we express true compassion. We become able to genuinely love, honor, and serve the common good without desire for reward.

Living in the center of the public eye, as most public leaders do, presents constant challenges to be consistent in choosing higher motives. It isn't difficult to make it appear as though we are acting on principle when, in fact, we may be secretly feeding certain ego needs. Politicians working primarily within Stage Two Traditionalism must constantly seek media opportunities that will allow them to stake claim on their good deeds as public servants. If a leader's primary objective is merely to remain in office, then his communication with the public he serves must be inundated with political spin to avoid negative repercussions. Now that the American media has become a 24-hour marathon, there is more opportunity than ever to toot one's political horn. The more politicians do this, however, the more their actions are based on achieving positive publicity, and the less real power they hold. Because all true empowerment proceeds from a foundation of higher motives, in order to rise to the level of greatest effectiveness, politicians must refuse to be baited by the seductive media mechanics of Traditional Stage Two politics.

> In order to rise to the level of greatest effectiveness, politicians must refuse to be baited by the seductive media mechanics of Traditional Stage Two politics.

Jesus spoke of a foolproof method for living from higher motives in his teaching about anonymous giving. In Matthew 6:3-4, Jesus' words are, "When you give alms, do not let your left hand know what your right hand is doing, so that your alms may be in secret." Giving to others anonymously enables us to remove any selfishness from the gift. This is true whether we are giving alms, or offering service.

I witnessed a poignant example of this lesson while working with a nonprofit organization. I was on a fundraising team, and one day we received a call from a potential donor. The staff person and I met with the donor and outlined a specific program to which he might contribute. At the end of the meeting he said, "I want to contribute $100,000 to the project, under one condition. Absolutely no one but the two of you are to know of this donation."

Of course we were wildly enthusiastic, but as the next few weeks unfolded I became skeptical of the man's motives—not due to anything he had said or done, but because I could not fathom anyone acting so generously without expecting personal recognition in return. My political fundraising experience had taught me that the powerful and wealthy want political candidates to know who has contributed to their cause. Giving anonymously would not increase their access and influence.

When the staff person and I went to the donor's home to pick up the check, we were met by the man and his wife together. Their questions indicated a sincere admiration for the program and genuine enthusiasm that their gift was going to make a difference. The two reminded us again that their gift was to remain absolutely anonymous. They asked us to keep them informed and to seek their assistance again if needed. These two people were interested only in sharing their gifts in a spirit of love and service. I left their home with tears in my eyes, moved by their gift of generosity and love. They had modeled for me one of the highest forms of service and of giving.

Since that time, I have noticed how easily my ego needs can become entangled with my desire to do good. I often convince myself that I am a Good Samaritan, ready and willing to save the world. If I look more deeply into my motives, however, I often find that, although I do want to be of service, I want just as much for others to see what a Good Samaritan I am! True service is an offering. An offering given in anticipation of recognition, however, ceases to be an offering and becomes merely a business transaction. The experience of these anonymous donors helped me to understand how giving anonymously can help to hold my desire for praise in check so that my service is offered freely and without expectation of reward.

Think about the actions you have taken while in a role of leadership. Would you have made the same decisions, would you have taken the same actions, had it been clear that those choices would not benefit you personally? If your answer is "no," if the appeal of being publicly congratulated played into your choices, then reconsider that time of leadership. How might you have protected yourself from acting in service of personal gain; how might you have approached the situation from a higher motive? In reconsidering my actions as a public leader, it helps me to remember the saying, "Character is what drives your actions when no one is looking."

> True service is an offering. An offering given in anticipation of recognition, however, ceases to be an offering and becomes merely a business transaction.

The writer and poet David Whyte says that service based upon higher motives means revealing ourselves. "To commit yourself to social action means you are making yourself visible, which means you are making yourself vulnerable." Our weaknesses may become exposed or open to attack. But when we merely serve our need to remain invulnerable to attack, we pay a heavy price. We become isolated and develop feelings of unworthiness. We perpetuate the cycle of desire for more goods or greater personal power, as our actions increasingly proceed not from a desire to serve but from an unquenchable hunger. We lose track of the deeper purpose of our lives.

In *Essential Spirituality,* Roger Walsh refers to cultivating higher motives as the basis of life. Before beginning one's period of daily meditation, he recommends repeating, "I dedicate my life to awakening, in order that I may serve and awaken all beings," or "I offer the benefits of my life to the welfare and awakening of all beings." Setting such an intention before you make a decision or head in a certain direction will transform your actions as a public leader. Repeating this intention before a meeting, a conversation, or a speech will alter your focus and seal your higher motivation. Dr. Walsh adds, "A central principle of both spirituality and psychology is that the more often we choose a particular motivation, the stronger it becomes."

I have found this technique of setting my intention to be helpful when I know I will be facing an angry audience or when I am called to speak on a difficult subject that is emotionally charged. Reminding myself *before the meeting* of my deepest motives for public service helps me to view people I disagree with or who may attack me in a more accepting light. When my motives are tangled in a desire for personal gain, I become defensive in such situations and unconsciously seek ways to make myself look good at the expense of others. Conversely, under the protection of my intention, I am less defensive and more readily able to hear opposing viewpoints.

Is Your Desire to Serve a *Calling* or a *Craving?*

In public life there is a thin line between the calling to serve and the craving to serve. Some of my clients report such a strong need to serve that it becomes a craving, kissing cousin to addiction. Those of us dedicated to public service sometimes confuse our desire to serve with a belief that we are supposed to serve. Our offering of service is then a craving rather than a calling.

A calling is a desire to give. A craving is a desire to get. A calling is our opportunity to share our unique contributions and blessings with others. A craving is a fear that there is not enough, a hole that we must fill. A calling arises naturally from our sense of completeness. A craving is a need to get more because we believe we are incomplete. A calling is a conscious awareness of our wholeness, spurring us to acts of spontaneous generosity. We know that by responding to our personal calling, by sharing our gifts in full, we encourage others to reveal their own greatness. A craving, on the other hand, is a nagging sense of lack, an unconscious reaction to an imagined deficit that demands to be overcome.

If we as public servants live with a craving to serve, many of the destructive by-products of addiction may arise in us: fear, manipulation, control, anger, jealousy, and excessive pride—the hallmarks of self-defeating behavior. Housing such toxic emotions, we become unable to listen to others. Our political approach turns mean-spirited, as our cravings gradually begin to run our lives for us. We may become so delusional that we believe we are destined to serve, that Someone on High has anointed our time in office. Our grandiosity grows, and we move into an all-out, self-centered power grab.

The seductive nature of public life, whether in the corporate world or in the arenas of sports and entertainment, may feed our cravings to hobnob with the rich and powerful. Hovering lobbyists, persons of privilege bidding for our attention, adoring staff, as well as plenty of alcohol and other drugs, all combine to make the public leader's life a fertile ground for cravings and addictions. Even healthy people who enter public life with their cravings under control often find that the pressures and temptations tend to magnify their cravings, sometimes even igniting full-blown addictions.

> Public leaders must be vigilant that our desire to do good does not become merely an acceptable cover for all that we crave.

Public leaders must be vigilant that the desire to do good does not become merely an acceptable cover for all that we crave. Reducing our cravings is a complex and demanding challenge. It often takes years to become aware of cravings and to become able to distinguish between a craving and a healthy desire. I am certainly not saying that there is anything wrong with having a desire to serve in office. Quite the contrary. I honor those who want to serve, who are willing to struggle with today's complex public issues. At the same time, it is important to know from whence you serve. Does your desire to serve come from a state of neediness, a craving? Or do you serve from a state of wholeness and balance? Do you feel alive and bursting with energy? Do your actions simply feel right? Are you naturally excited and do you often smile? Do you reserve judgment, listening openly and willingly to others when they offer you advice? Finding the answers to these questions for yourself will help you discern between the parts of your service that belong to your calling and the parts that belong to your craving. When you are living your true calling, the simple details of everyday life unfold in an authentic and harmonious way. It may be a messy and arduous process, one that does not necessarily happen according to your plans, but it is nevertheless filled with enthusiasm.

> If we can let go of our attachment to certain outcomes that serve our cravings, if we are willing to live with uncertainty, we will be free to live a life filled with selfless offerings, a life based on higher motives.

Living as a conscious public leader in tune with life's messages requires a different kind of listening. What is your life trying to tell you, right now, today? In this reflective space of asking and of listening, you'll find clues to your higher motives. As you consciously exercise patience, listening for possibility in the ordinary events of your life, becoming willing to learn and to trust, practicing gratitude—gradually you'll become able to discern with clarity your call to public leadership. Scott Peck, author of the classic *The Road Less Traveled*, says that there is no precise formula for knowing whether you are on your life's true path. He says, "The unconscious mind is always one step ahead of the conscious mind, so it's impossible to know for sure. But if you are willing to sit with ambiguity, to accept uncertainty and contradictory meanings, then your unconscious mind will always be a step ahead of your conscious mind in the right direction. You will therefore do the right thing, although you will not know it at the time."

Not surprisingly, powerful attachments, or cravings, are common in the world of public service. The lure of power, money, fame, and influence may distract us from our true passion and purpose. But if we can let go of our attachment to certain outcomes that serve our cravings, if we are willing to regularly enter with trust into a state of reflection, if we are willing to live with uncertainty, we will be free to live a life filled with selfless offerings, a life based on higher motives. When compassion and nonattachment guide our actions, our cravings won't stand a chance. Therein lies the true satisfaction of public service.

Recognizing the Assumption Beneath a Craving

I recently coached a candidate running for a visible city council position. He was smart, well spoken, knowledgeable, and deeply dedicated to public service. He had served on the planning commission and knew the complex city planning code inside and out. During our video practice session, this man appeared cold and uptight, giving me very little reason to vote for him. I decided to ask him a few questions.

"Dan, what is the most important characteristic you have, that you want the audience to know about you?"

He thought for a moment. "I am smart."

"How will the voters know you are smart?" I asked.

"They'll know I am smart enough to win this election."

"So if you lose the election, then are you dumb?" I countered.

"Well, not exactly." He paused. "Yes, I will be dumb if I lose. Or at least I will be *seen* as dumb because I couldn't win."

I asked, "Is that really true, that you are dumb if you lose?"

"There are a lot of good candidates in the race," he said. "Wanting everyone to know how smart I am is really crazy, isn't it?"

In that moment, he discovered the underlying assumption about his motives for running for office. Doing so helped him to choose whether he wanted to hold on to that motive for serving or shift to a higher motive. Having gotten a clear look at the thinking behind his decision to run, he said to himself, "That's really crazy," as we all do when we have a blinding flash of the obvious.

Understanding his underlying belief—that winning the city council race would mean that others would see him as smart—redirected this candidate's approach to his campaign. After a bit more conversation, he determined that he wanted to serve in order to address the more important issues facing his community, not merely to fill his own personal need. In just a few moments, his focus and his motives for serving underwent a dramatic shift. His face relaxed and he looked much more comfortable. He smiled as he spoke with a new sense of freedom and ease. This man easily won the election.

Examining the assumptions underlying your need to serve often gives access to your true motives. The more aware you are of the assumptions that drive your motives, the more naturally and powerfully you will speak and lead.

Relinquishing the Desire to Win

One of the surest ways to determine whether you are answering a calling to serve or a craving to serve is to relinquish your desire to win. To do this, visualize running for office and receiving the final election results. Picture what it would be like to lose the election. Now ask yourself:

How do I feel about the way I conducted myself
    during the campaign?
Did I stand up for what I believed in?
Did I treat my opponent with respect, as I
    would want to be treated?
Did I supervise my volunteers to ensure that they
    ran an ethical campaign?
Did I tell the truth about myself and my past?
Did I present my opponent's record fairly?

Even if you have never run for public office, you can do this exercise by remembering a time when you put forth a powerful argument in a meeting at work or in some other situation (even a conflict with a spouse). Imagine that you gave all your best examples, you spoke intelligently and made perfectly good sense in your approach, and yet your listener(s) continued to disagree with your position. You lost, despite your best efforts. Now ask yourself the questions above. Relinquishing your attachment to losing, making the win or loss beside the point, throws your attention onto what is most important: your motives. How did you conduct yourself in the campaign, or in the argument? Who were you as you put forth your opinion? Were you the kind of person you generally admire and respect, or were you someone you would rather avoid?

Time and again I have observed perfectly nice people who became ruthless candidates because they craved winning and put it first and foremost. To their own surprise and sometimes horror, they found themselves saying and doing things during their campaign (and while in office) that they would not ordinarily have done. The desire to win caused them to lose perspective and balance. Such obvious departures from our stated character ideals reveal a craving for power and influence rather than a calling to public service. I saw my own craving for winning when, as campaign manager in a governor's race, I thoughtlessly uttered that hurtful phrase, "May the best family win."

Right now you may be asking, "What kind of political leadership coach is she, if she advocates that her clients give up their goal of winning the election?" The stance of nonattachment certainly can appear to run counter to the objective of serving in office—or of simply making one's point in an argument, for that matter. After all, a candidate must win in order to serve, right? At this point I challenge you to consider two questions: *What does success mean to you? Does success consist only of winning the race, regardless of your personal conduct in the process?*

> When candidates release their strong attachment to winning, they liberate themselves from the fear of losing.

When candidates release their strong attachment to winning, they liberate themselves from the fear of losing. Unrestricted by fear, they become free to speak and lead in more powerful ways. A position of nonattachment yields new energy that fuels a leader's passion to speak the truth. And nothing is more attractive, more irresistible, than a passion for truth.

What Do You Want to Contribute?

One of the best ways to avoid the negative politics of domination is to be absolutely clear about the contribution you want to make. I have observed that public figures often are not crystal clear about what they want to contribute and to whom they want to offer their service. They may enter politics with a vague sense of their intent to contribute, then they win an election or two and suddenly life on the public treadmill has begun. Without a clear focus, their entire career quickly becomes trained on seeking political media opportunities rather than on bringing their contribution into being.

> The object of the game for you now is to make your contribution rather than to defeat those who disagree with you.

Such public leaders listen almost solely to their political consultants and pollsters, as their vision for the future shrinks to no further than the next election. Such public servants feel constantly stymied, never fully understanding what they are doing in public service or where they want to go. Balance is lost and higher motives swept aside. Their efforts are given to winning reelection rather than savoring their time in office as an opportunity to serve.

When I ask my clients why they are running for office, they frequently answer, "I want to make a difference in the world." It is a general statement, an undeveloped vision. It takes considerable time, conversation, and depth of personal reflection before most public figures are able to clearly state the specific contribution that they intend to make. The more specifically a candidate or public servant is able to articulate her intention for serving, the more easily she will marshal the energy and heart to make her intention a reality.

When you declare your intention to contribute to the world, to make a difference, you have decided to share your gifts. Your time in public leadership becomes a contribution game rather than a game of winning or losing. Your focus shifts. The object of the game for you now is to make your contribution rather than to defeat those who disagree with you.

The more eager we are to serve with compassion, to contribute to the lives of other people the easier it is for us to see the value of others, and to understand the crucial part they play in the world. We can look to Mother Teresa as a beautiful case in point. Throughout her life of service to the orphans and lepers, the dying and forgotten on the streets of Calcutta, she often said that she served Jesus "in the distressing disguise of the poorest of the poor." She asked nothing from those she served, but offered love and care to each one with compassionate generosity. Though she herself was only one humble woman, her humanitarian efforts grew by leaps and bounds because her love of spirit and her contribution were beyond measure.

We do not have to be Mother Teresa in order to serve with love. To practice the Politics of Hope we can commit to living life in service of higher motives rather than in service of our cravings— our short-term ego needs. When we ask, "How may I contribute?" we point ourselves toward our true calling. If we refuse the call to service, we will feel stuck because we are denying the world our true gifts. To stand in a position of true power, we must acknowledge our calling and become willing to do what it takes to offer our gifts in service to the collective good.

Coaching Questions

Taking time for reflection will allow you to discern the difference between a craving and a calling. Long walks, journaling, prayer, meditation—contemplative moments that allow you to listen to your true self—are essential if you are to become aware of your deepest motives. You might ask yourself:

1. Will I remain unfulfilled if I do not obtain this position or office?
2. If I do not serve in public office or land this job, will my life still have meaning and purpose?
3. Does this office or public position define who I am?
4. Imagine that you're reading the headline of your own obituary. In a few words, the headline captures the major contribution you made in your lifetime. How does the headline read?

9

Sharing Your Unique Gifts

You are not here by accident. You made it to Earth. You penetrated the egg. That suggests you are great and unique. Do not tell children to be another Martin Luther King. Let them be who God placed them on the Earth to be.

—Reverend Bernice King
Daughter of Martin Luther King Jr.

The great 21st century public leaders who will lead us through the chaos of our times will be those who do three things very well:

1. They are aware of their unique gifts.
2. They cultivate and nurture these gifts.
3. They choose to share their gifts with the world.

Embracing and fostering your unique gifts takes courage, even audacity. It means acknowledging to yourself and others that you are here to fully engage in the world. Before you can share your gifts, however, you must first become aware of them. Then you must consciously choose to share them, not for your own aggrandizement but to be of service, to offer what you were put here on Earth to contribute. After that, you must make a life practice of cultivating and nurturing your gifts (See chapter 10, "Cultivating Your Political Habitat").

Great leaders do not necessarily start out intending to become great leaders. They become great leaders because they are passionate about motivating others to become involved, to give their best; for this reason others naturally look to them for leadership and inspiration. People want to follow a leader who shares freely of herself and encourages others to do the same. Successful public leaders do not shrink from what they have to offer, instead they dig deep into the psyche and heart in an attempt to understand their own God-given creativity. They live in a constant effort to make their distinctive offerings to the world, always seeking to ensure that their contributions are of real and lasting service.

What Purpose?

Leading from higher motives means we are called to give rather than to get. When we lead from a place of giving, we instinctively share our gifts in the process. We want to give what we have to offer; it becomes the moving force in our lives. In this process of giving, we also discover that each and every human being has unique gifts to share with the world. Stage Four Conscious Public Leaders draw everyone into the collaborative process. We look at a chaotic situation and see an irresistible opportunity for growth. We know that through successful collaboration, order can be wrought out of chaos. With enthusiasm and determination, we seek to include many others in the transformation process. We know that great change requires more than a tenacious team of one.

> Successful public leaders do not shrink from what they have to offer, instead they dig deep into the psyche and heart in an attempt to understand their own God-given creativity.

In chapter 7 we looked at the importance of discovering the spiritual center, the source of true guidance, that rests within all of us. Then (in chapter 8) we considered how service based on higher motives frees us from a self-centered approach to life and catapults us into genuine concern for the collective good. Becoming aware of our spiritual orientation, serving our highest principles, and choosing to share our unique gifts is a recipe for a life of leadership. We can also think of it as an equation.

Spiritual Orientation + Higher Motives + Unique Gifts = Life Purpose

These three elements lead us to our life purpose, that distinctive awareness deep inside that gives our life meaning. The modern literature of self-help overflows with advice about where and how to discover one's life purpose because we all have the desire to understand why we are on this earth. Learning more about our reason for living is a universal endeavor. However, unless we choose to share our innate gifts in some way, the realization of our life purpose will not benefit anyone, not even ourselves. We may explore our spiritual nature and feel firmly rooted in higher motives, and yet if we keep our gifts hidden under the bed, who will be enriched by their beauty? What meaning will they have contributed? To complete the equation of our life purpose, we must have not only a spiritual orientation and awareness of higher motives, we must also complete the courageous final step: fully embracing our gifts and sharing them with the world.

Why Our Gifts Matter

It matters greatly that we share our unique gifts: it paves the way for others to do the same. Because the new collaborative leadership model requires the full participation of the many, our courage in expressing our gifts is more important than ever. When the hierarchical (top-down) leadership paradigm was the only practical model of leadership, the dominators at the top of the authority chain called all the shots. Employees or supporters, those on the lower rungs of the hierarchy, were not asked for their opinions, regardless of how valuable their knowledge might be. Inclusive participation was almost nonexistent, and speaking up or offering uninvited input might even cost you your job. Fortunately, increased awareness of the value of collaboration and diversity in business organizations, academic circles, and religious institutions has made it popular to broaden the base of participation.

When I served as a state legislator, I sponsored what is commonly referred to as whistle-blower legislation to protect state workers who spoke out publicly against fraud, waste, or other important issues that could compromise the integrity of government. This legislation created a safety net for state workers so they were free to speak up, sharing with management and other workers about policies and practices that needed to be changed. Encouraging honest and open communication in the work environment is another way of valuing the unique perspectives and contributions of workers. Taking apart the top-down model so that people may more truly cooperate, honorably working toward a common end—whether it's making widgets or making laws—is only one example of the way in which new leadership paradigms are changing the world.

In another example of the new move toward inclusion, religious lay ministers now help determine the administrative direction of many churches. While the level of their inclusion varies from church to church, in almost all religions lay ministers are more involved in church leadership than ever before. No longer a passive congregation of spectators, lay persons have become active movers in their own religious lives. Likewise, in the world of commerce successful business leaders are including workers in what used to be considered executive decision-making, having discovered that honoring the contributions of employees increases worker morale and commitment, which in turn improves the company's bottom line. In short, everyone wins.

Collaboration has the power to reinvigorate true servant leadership in our country, thereby reviving our dream of real democracy. But it is an essential element of this new collaborative paradigm that no leader can succeed unless he does so on behalf of—in service of—the collective good. Rejuvenating our democracy, making it relevant in the 21st century, therefore, means garnering the full participation of the people, by the people, and for the people. If this has a familiar ring, there's a good reason.

The Shadow Side of Sharing Our Gifts

Leaders can't be trusted to say *yes* unless we can be trusted to say *no*. If you can't say *no*, then your *yes* doesn't carry much weight. The power of the small word *no* is embedded in the idea that all human beings have limits. Those of us who love a fast-paced lifestyle filled with multi tasking seem to produce better when we're perched on the precipice of a deadline, with our toes planted right on the edge of overwhelm. This is my own tendency; I say *yes* to nearly everything, and the resulting pressure creates a certain focus that allows me to accomplish quite a lot! The "I'm so busy" lifestyle has a built-in danger, however, because it tends to shove out time for reflection: the crucial journeying deeper into our spiritual center, from whence true inspiration springs. As we grow older, saying *yes* to every possible opportunity and obligation ends up draining our energy, and ultimately it compromises our most important relationships, not to mention our

> Rejuvenating our democracy, making it relevant in the 21st century, therefore, means garnering the full participation of the people, by the people, and for the people. If this has a familiar ring, there's a good reason.

relationship with ourselves.

The power of saying *no* creates boundaries for our lives. It works in much the same way that a stable riverbank keeps a river contained and flowing in a way that provides habitat for fish, transportation for boats, and water that farmers may use to nourish their crops. If we neglect to say *no*, if we do not maintain our appropriate limits, then like a flooding river, not only do we lose control, but those nourished and supported by our activity are hurt: fish die, boats run aground, crops dry up. Staying within our natural limits by saying *no* to whatever is too much for us, to whatever might flood our lives and create chaos, is an essential practice for the conscious public leader.

> Leaders can't be trusted to say *yes* unless we can be trusted to say *no.*

Some leaders have a habit of oversharing their gifts, which denies others the opportunity to participate. The ego is always eager to conclude that we should just do it ourselves. This internal voice seduces us into believing that we know best. In accord with this line of thinking, it seems easier to exclude others, take charge, and take over. All we want is to get the job done, and since we already know what needs to be done, we proceed without benefit of the help or input of others. This dynamic destroys the collaborative process and, in very short order, creates an addictive overworking syndrome. The healthy habit of saying *no* at appropriate times conserves our energy and invites others to pitch in.

The personality trait that encourages leaders to take risks by choosing public participation is closely related to the trait that encourages them to dominate a meeting, talk a bit too much, and vie to be the center of attention. These expressions of personal power comprise the dark or shadow side of sharing our gifts. If we have convinced ourselves that we are more special than everyone else, it is hard to accept that creative solutions might come from others; we expect others to listen to our plans and unquestioningly follow our lead. This is the old top-down leadership style, and it sabotages effective collaboration—the backbone of conscious public leadership.

In *The Art of Possibility,* Benjamin and Rosamund Zander discuss the idea of balancing our lives: knowing when to share our gifts, and when to listen and lighten up. They call it "Rule Number 6," and they tell the following humorous story to illustrate.

> Two prime ministers are sitting in a room discussing affairs of state. Suddenly a man bursts in, apoplectic with fury, shouting and stamping and banging his fist on the desk. The resident prime minister admonishes him: "Peter," he says, "kindly remember Rule Number 6," whereupon Peter is instantly restored to complete calm, apologizes, and withdraws. The politicians return to their conversation, only to be interrupted yet again twenty minutes later by an hysterical woman gesticulating wildly, her hair flying. Again the intruder is greeted with the words: "Marie, please remember Rule Number 6." Complete calm descends once more, and she too withdraws with a bow and an apology. When the scene is repeated a third time, the visiting prime minister addresses his colleague: "My dear friend, I have seen many things in my life, but never anything as remarkable as this. Would you be willing to share with me the secret of Rule Number 6?" "Very simple," replies the resident prime minister. "Rule Number 6 is "Don't take yourself so g--damn seriously." "Ah," says his visitor, "that is a fine rule." After a moment of pondering, he inquires, "And what, may I ask, are the other rules?" "There aren't any."

Conscious public leaders must master the delicate balance of knowing when to take charge and when to be quiet and listen, thereby subtly encouraging others to lead. When we don't take ourselves so seriously, we can be fully involved in public issues while maintaining the awareness that while we have much to share, we also have much to learn from others.

In order to keep our spiritual center, we must work to serve from higher motives, and we must take action to put both our spiritual inspiration and our principles to practical use. Otherwise, our gifts languish in secret and no one benefits. If we've done the soul-searching necessary to clarify our gifts, if we have done what we must do to press those gifts into service of higher goals, we stand at the gateway of the realization of our life purpose. To construct a foundation to manifest our highest goals of conscious public leadership, we must now build our ideal Political Habitat. In the next chapter, we'll explore ways to do just that.

Coaching Exercise and Questions

Creating Your Gift List

1. Take just a few minutes, sit down in a comfortable place with a pen and paper, and prepare your own Gift List: a list of your attributes, talents, and abilities. Spend a minimum of five minutes and write every gift that comes to your mind. Do not allow your internal critic to filter your unique gifts. Just write. Remember Rule Number 6: Lighten up and don't take yourself too seriously. Consider all your unique gifts, leaving nothing out. You may have a warm smile that brings a smile to others—that's a gift. You may be good at public speaking—that's a gift, too. Be sure to include often-overlooked personal traits that promote collaboration, such as being a good listener, being curious, or

asking questions that others might avoid.

2. Put your Gift List aside for a day or two. When you read it again, be open to embracing your many gifts. Begin thinking about how you will share your gifts with the world. No more hiding!

3. What higher motive (generosity, belief in the power of unity, service, compassion) supports you in sharing your gifts?

4. If you don't share your gifts, what will the world have lost?

10

Cultivating Your Political Habitat

At any moment, you have a choice, that either leads
you closer to your spirit or further away from it.

—Thich Nhat Hanh

Becoming aware of our unique gifts and deciding to share them are essential first steps in cooperating with our own political evolution. To revive our democracy, however, means bringing the Politics of Hope into being in our own lives. To do this we must take another step, because getting in touch with our gifts and being willing to use them is only the beginning. We live in a rapidly evolving age. In this age, conscious public leaders are lifelong learners who choose to cultivate our gifts: always growing, improving, and learning. Our persistence in evolving our understanding keeps us ahead of the chaos curve. Such enlightened public leaders consciously create an ideal political habitat for ourselves—an inner state of being in which we find guidance, refuge, and wisdom regarding any challenge, personal or political.

A *habitat* is defined as a place or environment where a living organism naturally grows and thrives. In the Pacific Northwest where I live, we are familiar with the plight of the salmon whose extraordinary life cycle drives them to the original habitat where they were spawned. After swimming downstream and feeding in the ocean, adult salmon return as adults to their original habitat, the precise location at which their lives began. If the fish cannot complete their journey properly—if the streams are muddy, polluted, or impassable for other reasons—the salmon's life cycle is disrupted. Without benefit of their native vegetation, the correct balance of shade and sun, or woody debris in which to hide from predators, these salmon eggs simply do not hatch. Without a safe and nourishing habitat, the salmon may not survive.

The same holds true for the life cycle of our democracy: it requires a habitat appropriate to nourishing new conscious public leaders who can lead us through the chaos we are facing in the 21st century. If we do not create a political habitat that nourishes the notion of equal regard for self and others, we cannot expect to witness the emergence of new leaders who hold this strong conviction. If we create a political habitat for ourselves that naturally encourages our own virtues to grow and thrive, the next generation of conscious public leaders, too, will be encouraged and empowered by our example. Our dream of real democracy will be revived.

> If we create a political habitat for ourselves that naturally encourages our virtues to thrive, the next generation will be empowered by our example.

A plant or animal habitat includes a myriad of necessary environmental elements: clean air, water, and proper food, as well as refuge from dangerous predators and harmful weather. Unlike the Pacific Northwest salmon, human beings have a choice about where we live, what we eat, and the company we keep. We are the only species in the history of the world with the freedom to choose our own habitat! So the question arises: What are the qualities of a habitat that nurtures our growth as leaders? What are the elements of our habitat that distract us from higher motives? Does our choice of friends and acquaintances produce toxic situations that move us away from our spiritual center, or do our associations contribute a greater vision of our virtues? After we have determined our unique gifts and have made a firm decision to use those gifts in service to the collective good, we must create a political habitat for ourselves that supports our goal. Consciously choosing our own political habitat—the environment in which we and other public leaders can survive and thrive as servants of higher motives—is the next Essential Practice for becoming a conscious public leader.

Choosing Your Political Habitat

Great leaders choose a political habitat that cultivates their gifts and helps them share those gifts generously in the world. To do this successfully, it helps to bear three things in mind at all times:

1. While leading and expressing your gifts, remain open to new learning.
2. Listen to feedback from your habitat as to what is nurturing and what is not.
3. Remember that the quality of feedback is based on the quality of your habitat.

Just as in the plant and animal kingdoms, our habitat determines how heartily our species is expressed on this earth. As a political leadership coach, I challenge my clients to aspire to do more than merely survive. For an elected public leader, survival may only mean winning the next election. As a coach, however, I urge leaders to do whatever it takes to really *thrive*. Conscious public leadership means going far beyond simple survival, into the realm of expansive and visionary living. The quality of your habitat has the power to determine how you are as a public leader. Your political habitat can keep you bogged down in familiar problems and old ways of considering them, or it can open you up to new information, giving you fresh perspectives on old problems. Your political habitat is one of the most powerful elements in your effort to lead and to serve responsibly.

The old top-down (hierarchical) leadership model that previously dominated business, religion, law, and health care, meant that power rested with a tiny few. It was a political habitat that spawned a great number of political leaders who now thrive in today's highly partisan, opponent-crushing power politics. We don't have to look far in history to see how quickly the change from top-down leadership to cooperative collaboration has occurred. In the 1960s women rarely held credit cards in their own names and could not make purchases without their husband's signatures. Members of minorities were "redlined" from receiving bank loans that would allow them to own homes and go into business. The dominate-or-perish model that kept a handful of people on top and others in a position of subjugation has been our only model of leadership and decision-making throughout most of history.

Will our democratic system ignore the cultural landscape that is spawning so much rapid change in the rest of our society? Our political evolution, and thus the evolution of our leadership style, is now hurling us into the future at Mach speed. Because we are the only species, plant or animal, with the ability to choose our habitat, we bear the responsibility for the future of our species. If we don't make it, it's nobody else's fault. The habitat choices we make, as individuals and as a society, will determine our future. How we live, where, and with whom has never been more important.

Ralph Waldo Emerson consciously chose to live and write near his beloved Walden Pond. He found great solitude in nature and discovered a habitat that supported his creative and intellectual pursuits. While Emerson lived in Concord, Massachusetts, his presence attracted other great poets and writers: Henry Wadsworth Longfellow, Nathaniel Hawthorne, Louisa May Alcott and Herman Melville. They gathered in their homes, took long walks together, and laid a foundation of creative community and intellectual discourse that later became a habitat for some of our country's most esteemed American poets and writers.

By sheer force of proximity and constant engagement, these American writers grew in affection for each other. Their collective support of each other gave them each a sense of contribution to something greater than their individual goals and personal concerns. Through conversation, debate, and discourse, Emerson and his colleagues consciously cultivated their ideas, giving birth to the influential Transcendental philosophy of the 19th century. Word spread that a conclave of great minds was to be found in Concord, and young writers flocked to the area. These literati, both the elders and the youthfully exuberant, together spawned one of the greatest philosophical movements in American history. The rise of the Transcendentalists is a living example of a successful political habitat. It was a habitat that arose in an era of change, and it also helped great evolutionary change to come to pass.

It is an unavoidable fact that the quality of your habitat will determine the quality of feedback you receive from your environment. If you rarely venture out from your personal perspective, you'll receive very little feedback from your habitat. In the business and political world, we often hear of leaders who surround themselves with people and circumstances that screen out any information that might challenge the validity of their existing points of view. This policy of habitat management may allow such leaders to survive in the short run; however, they will not thrive, nor will they encourage others to thrive. Conscious public leaders are courageous, unafraid to have our existing views disrupted and rearranged. We cultivate curiosity, maintain a welcoming attitude toward possibility, and invite new ideas. The human spirit instinctively longs for stimulation, learning, and exploration. If your habitat closes options, reduces possibilities, and allows for association only with others who think as you do, you will shrink in fear when a truly original thought comes your way.

Being comfortable with a certain set of political ideas only confirms what we already know. Comfort keeps us bound in place, isolated and unable to walk in someone else's shoes. By actively seeking to move out of our comfort zone, we stretch and grow: we evolve as political beings. Unlike other members of the animal kingdom who might die if they stray too far from their natural environment, human beings can choose to venture further into unknown territory, to envision what lies ahead. Humanity, however, is also nonessential.

Consider this humbling fact: We are the only creatures on this planet without which Earth could survive and thrive. Therefore we must be open to considering in which habitat we may live the most balanced, conscious life on Earth. As we contemplate, we may find ourselves taking a much larger political view than we're accustomed to.

Consider someone you know who holds a political point of view that varies sharply from your own. Ask yourself what the circumstances might have been which led to that approach. Conscious public leaders work to remain open to others' positions; we seek to understand and listen because our focus is primarily on living honorably, not living for a certain outcome. As conscious leaders we enjoy lively discourse that encourages intellectual discovery and personal growth. More interested in these than in our personal comfort, conscious public leaders invite friends, fellow workers, and other associates to challenge our line of thinking and to question our assumptions.

Whatever Your Focus, That's What You Create

Cultivating a nourishing political habitat begins with our focus. What we dwell on literally "becomes us." Philosopher and psychologist William James said, "The faculty of voluntarily bringing back a wandering attention, over and over again, is the root of judgment, character and will." James went on to say, "Each of us literally chooses, by the ways of attending to things, what sort of universe he shall appear to himself to inhabit." James is saying that whatever we give our attention to is what we create in our lives. As conscious public leaders we must cultivate a tremendous strength of focus, keeping our attention riveted on living the highest principles, to ensure that whatever we create will be beneficial to all of humanity.

Many of us pride ourselves on multi tasking and working well in chaotic, high-pressure situations. Such skills serve us well in maintaining our hectic pace, but they can also prevent us from developing the art of discrimination. We must be able to listen and decide. As we stop to hear our internal political noise, we must decide whether we are present, alive in the moment and in our bodies, or whether, at this moment, we are unconscious to our true nature. To do this, however, we must first be aware that we

> Conscious public leaders must cultivate a tremendous strength of focus...to ensure that whatever they create will be beneficial to all of humanity.

have an inner life to listen to! Calming the mind with regular periods of contemplation, prayer, journal writing, meditation, or yoga, or by other means, allows us to listen within.

Our true passions always want to come forward to be heard. A political habitat that nurtures our goodness of spirit through solitude and time for reflection naturally gives rise to a wise mind and a compassionate heart. Our compulsive, multi tasking tendency works in the reverse, making us more susceptible to fear, manipulation and a compulsion to control. We may choose a habitat filled with associates who share these destructive traits. Conversely, a quiet, focused mind is also open and receptive, and quite naturally creates a habitat that nourishes our health and our highest goals. In this state of hope and peace, we attract into our habitat other people who, like ourselves, are less burdened by toxic habits.

Political Gossip

A wise person once said, "Conversation is an exercise of the mind, but gossiping is merely an exercise of the tongue." Probably the most destructive feature in anyone's political habitat is the presence of gossip. Conscious public leaders understand the disharmony created by a lazy tongue, and they avoid gossip as a matter of grave necessity. The habit of gossip is insidious and can quickly pollute our political habitat to the point that it threatens our greatest intentions and our most dearly held principles.

The word gossip was originally *godsibba*, meaning "god sibling," and referred to the four godparents (usually two married couples) who were present at the baptism of a child and who pledged to look after the child's spiritual well-being. Godsibbas got together periodically to talk about the welfare and spiritual progress of the child, and the term *godsib* came to mean "talk among equals." The word later evolved into today's spelling: gossip.

The Oxford English Dictionary gives the first instance of the word *godsib* (or *godzyb*) in writing as 1014: "One who has contracted spiritual affinity with another by acting as a sponsor at a baptism." By 1566, one's *gossips*, used as a noun, were "a woman's female friends invited to be present at a baptism," and soon the verb form had come to mean "easy, unrestrained talk or writing, about persons or social incidents." During the past five centuries, *gossip* lost both its spiritual meaning and its positive connotation as talk among equals to support the welfare of another.

I wish we could reclaim the original meaning of the word *gossip*. Today, vicious political gossip is an art form spun by individuals and groups wanting to do harm. Conscious public leaders must create a political habitat that protects them from these destructive energies.

Political Noise

Political noise is the collection of assumptions built into our current political system—the "we've-always-done-it-this-way" that prevents us from entertaining new political possibilities. It amounts to annoying background static. Rather than continue to listen, we simply screen out the speaker's message. It's similar to the way in which millions of Americans have decided to ignore politics. The political noise we subject ourselves to can be so subtle that we don't realize how profoundly it affects us.

Consider this longtime rule of partisan politics: One member of a party should not endorse a member of the opposite party. This is only one of many "rules of the game" that prevent us from working together collaboratively and from discovering new ways of handling our challenges. If we're both hearing a lot of political noise and also taking in all that static from others—the critical voices of the status quo—how can we hope to hear a new message of hope? In such a climate, how can we revive the dream of democracy? Listen for a moment:

That's just the way it is.
What good does it do to fight the system?
Things will never change.

That's the sound of political noise. There is another kind of political noise: the internal kind. This political noise takes place in the mind, filling it with an agitating chatter that, left unchecked, can prevent us from taking action to support the changes our heart desires. I experienced this kind of political noise the first time I caught sight of a 20-foot billboard with my name on it.

It was the spring of 1978, and I was running for my party's nomination for the Oregon State House of Representatives. Of course, I was well aware that our campaign budget included six billboards in my district—I had approved the artwork myself and knew the location of the billboard. So I shouldn't have been surprised to see my name in gigantic letters as I drove my car down the main highway in town. Nevertheless, I slammed on my brakes and swerved off the highway, almost causing an accident— all because I had seen my name in lights.

In an instant, I realized the internal political noise to which I was responding by swerving off the road: *All politicians are crooks! And my name is on a billboard, therefore, I'm one of them!* As far as my internal noise was concerned, the sign might as well have read, "Donna Zajonc for Dishonesty." I felt exposed in the worst sort of way. Until that moment, I would never have guessed that somewhere deep down, I had accepted the political noise of American culture that incessantly babbles, "Politicians are crooked." Suddenly I realized why I had so often found myself *apologizing* for wanting to serve in the legislature. I realized why my campaign speeches lacked a sense of purpose and belief in what I could accomplish.

At that point, it wasn't merely that I had some political noise: it had me. This internal chatter—of which I was for the most part unaware—was keeping me from having a bigger and much better conversation within myself. Whether we know it or not, we all have limiting assumptions, political background noise that works against us. We must become aware of these pressures before we can be free to make conscious choices about who we want to associate with, before we can construct a political habitat conducive to hope. Once we distinguish our noisy self-chatter, we have the power to decide whether we want to continue listening or to steer the conversation in a more fruitful direction.

Whether our political noise comes from our internal voices or from the cultural pressures of society, we must be vigilant to catch it in action. There is so much political background noise at this point in time that many potentially great leaders don't even want to consider reengaging in the public conversation—especially not as elected public servants. But if we are to rejuvenate our democracy, we must turn our attention to the quieter voice of hope, shifting our attention away from political noise and focusing it on our inner inspiration.

In *Leadership and the Art of Conversation,* Kim Krisco speaks to the importance of mastering "background conversations." He asserts that by becoming aware of and managing the broad, invisible background conversations that determine the way we see and interpret the world—our political noise—we can then decide whether we want to live in the past or create a new point of view. That new point of view may be so powerful, so compelling, that it becomes the foundation of our public leadership message. But this can only happen if we are able to hear it through the static of the political noise in the background.

The political habitat you build for yourself must include an awareness of this background noise and the effect it has on you. Associate with positive people whose sense of hope is alive, who honor the power of reviving the dream of democracy. Talk with and listen to people who still dare to believe in our political system, those who continue to insist that we can and will improve the way we do the people's business. Leave cynicism behind, unlock your radio dial, and tune in to new possibilities.

Coaching Questions

1. Make a list of the features of your political habitat that nurture your sense of purpose and service to humanity. What can you do that will help you create an even more nurturing habitat?

2. What kinds of distractions exist in your political habitat that you are willing to remove?

3. Be honest about your intake of mood-altering substances that may interfere with your best functioning.

4. Name at least two people you know whose lives and choices inspire you. Commit to spending time with them, personally, by phone, or by e-mail.

5. Write down the name of one literary mentor whose writing inspires you. Commit to reading his (or her) work.

6. What kind of exercise would best nurture your ideal political habitat?

7. Do you get adequate rest? If not, what changes can you make to ensure that this fundamental need is addressed? A tired leader is an ineffective leader!

8. Do your reading choices reflect habit, or do they arise from adventurous curiosity and a willingness to try on different perspectives? Consider reading one magazine or newspaper a week that you might not ordinarily read. Be open to a genuine understanding of the opposing point of view.

11

Communicating with Integrity and Trust

Democracy begins in conversation.

> —Philosopher John Dewey
> on his 90th birthday

As conscious public leaders we keep our word. We know that our authority is derived from doing what we say and saying what we do. Even if you diligently devoured the first four Essential Practices for becoming a conscious public leader—(1) finding your spiritual center, (2) leading based upon higher motives, (3) becoming aware of your unique gifts, and (4) cultivating your political habitat—all that good work will fall away if your voice is not in alignment with your values.

Great communicators are not born that way—they grow into it. They develop their communication skills as a result of deep desire, focused study, and constant practice. Individuals with natural public speaking skills may captivate us, only to disappoint us later when we discover that their message was a fraud. Charismatic and dynamic speakers, no matter how entertaining they are, cannot maintain our confidence if they do not speak with integrity. Only the individual who has done her internal work, who speaks in alignment with her highest ideals and actions, will earn the highest honor that we the people can bestow: our trust.

Speaking with integrity begins on the inside. What we say to ourselves is our first and most important conversation. Only after we understand our own internal conversation—with all the foibles and strengths it reveals to us—are we ready to enter the public conversation consciously. Thus, the process of developing a public voice of integrity consists of five steps.

1. Keeping commitments to yourself and to others.
2. Understanding and seeing current reality.
3. Developing the skill of listening.
4. Learning the art of asking questions and living in possibility.
5. Relinquishing the notion that others are right or wrong.

A conscious public leader must be able to communicate with ease. For him, the art of public speaking must not seem artful, but natural. To anyone serious about public leadership, I recommend hiring a public speaking coach or joining organizations such as Toastmasters International where you may practice speaking publicly. Receiving constructive feedback will dramatically improve your speaking skills in a matter of months. Public speaking is an ever-evolving learning process. If you approach gaining skill in public speaking as vigorously as you would approach any other important task, your effort will be rewarded. In time you will be able to speak naturally and spontaneously—while making your point—to a group of any size.

> Speaking with integrity begins on the inside. What we say to ourselves is our first and most important conversation.

Communicating with integrity, however, is an *inside job*. For this reason, the practices I recommend in this section have more to do with your heart and soul than with your ability to memorize a set of bullet points on an index card. No amount of practice or training will help you speak with heart and authenticity. By definition, these are qualities that can't be faked. First you must do the inner work that develops an inner culture of integrity.

Keeping Commitments to Yourself and Others

Like many others, you may avoid making commitments for fear that you will not follow through. You may fear that you'll be pressured into doing something you don't want to do. From this viewpoint, making a commitment can feel like a burden, a threat to your flexibility or independence. Indulging your commitment phobia gives the illusion that you remain free to explore and to go with the flow.

The fact is, however, that we make commitments every day—to our children and other loved ones, to our colleagues, neighbors, and friends. The agreement may be as simple as picking up our children from school on time or as life-changing as a decision to marry. Such agreements smooth out the bumps of living in cooperation with others. Keeping our agreements, with ourselves as well as with others, forms the basis of integrity.

I once attended a workshop that emphasized the powerful link between keeping commitments and building personal integrity. Frankly, I was anxious going in. I worried that in order to maintain my trustworthiness I might have to make even more commitments, and as usual, I had quite a lot on my plate. The workshop hadn't even begun, and I was already overwhelmed! During the course of the day, however, I made an important discovery. Although as a rule I was extremely diligent about keeping my word to others, I often reneged on my commitments to myself. If I made a promise to someone else, I would move mountains—not out of a sense of joyful service but to avoid disapproval—to keep from letting others down. When it came to my personal commitments, the ones I had made to myself, I often let things slide. I wasn't being honest with myself; I was saying one thing to myself and then doing another. I wasn't being entirely honest with others, either. My reason for keeping my promises was secretly fear-based, not service-based.

Often we tell ourselves that we will cut back on the cookies or that we'll exercise five days a week, only to discover that we don't follow through. Our agreements with ourselves are like so much water running off our backs. Little by little we learn not to trust the commitments we make to ourselves. We become a little cynical and find it harder to respect ourselves. When breaking our word to ourselves becomes easy, it's a short walk to breaking our word to others. We tell ourselves that they won't find out or that everyone tells little white lies. We make up excuses for our lateness to meetings, justify making extra copies at work for personal use. These examples may seem trivial, but they are the first symptoms that we are losing our integrity.

In the world of construction, integrity is foremost. It's a practical matter: if a building isn't well-built, if it doesn't have structural integrity, the first earth tremor will bring it down. In a building that has structural integrity, the walls are sturdy and strong. The internal beams are huge timbers, brawny enough to hold up the building's own weight, to support its inhabitants, and to meet the challenges presented by all manner of weather. Yet even massive wooden beams assembled by master carpenters can be demolished, little by little, by a persistent band of tiny termites. It may take years for the insects to do it, but eventually they will conquer the building's structural integrity, and the whole thing will come crashing to the ground. In the same way, our little white lies to ourselves and to others eat away at our integrity. Those tiny falsehoods and seemingly insignificant broken promises not only jeopardize the quality of our public leadership, they undermine the quality of our lives.

If we do not keep our personal commitments to ourselves, if we hide our true motives for doing what we do, we devalue ourselves. Not keeping the agreements we make to ourselves plants a seed of distrust in ourselves, in turn reducing the likelihood that we will follow through and keep our commitments to others. The result is that we become either (a) a person who avoids commitments and thus has great difficulty creating trusting relationships, or (b) a person who makes commitments while secretly believing she won't follow through; this ultimately requires us to fabricate excuses for breaking our promises. We acquire a habit of stretching the truth and putting a favorable spin on our statements to cover our falsehoods. Either way, we have seriously damaged our personal integrity. The façade may look good for awhile, as long as the compromised structure holds, but before long it becomes obvious that our castle is built on quicksand.

Integrity and honesty are two of the words most frequently bandied about in the literature of political campaigns. In light of the recent corporate scandals, we are especially sensitive to the need for honesty in public life. The person who must speak about honesty in order to convince others of his high level of integrity becomes suspect. A person rarely speaks about her integrity or honesty unless she is having trouble convincing herself that her motives are honor-

> If you keep the commitments you make to yourself, you will naturally keep the commitments you make to others.

able. The most sophisticated spin is no substitute for authenticity. We gain our credibility, our authority in life, not only by what we say but also by our example.

What is the degree of your internal integrity? Do you keep the agreements you make with yourself? The psyche is a powerful tool. When that power is dedicated to living in alignment with your word, it not only upholds the integrity of your character, but it also acts as a bright beacon for others. Public leaders must constantly work with other people to conduct negotiations, to apply policy, and to make all manner of decisions affecting the public. Making and keeping agreements is essential to gain others' trust in such situations, which are often laced with conflict. If you keep the commitments you make to yourself, you will naturally keep the commitments you make to others. Decision making becomes easier: you do not have to remember what you told others because it is the same message you told yourself, and your actions are in line with what you say. When you feel naturally empowered by your own personal internal integrity, you learn to trust yourself.

Seeing Reality as It Is

Keeping personal commitments to yourself and others does little good if it is based upon fantasy. I may promise to pick up my daughter from school at four pm, but if her school day ends at three what good is my promise? My commitment is not based in reality.

Today's media is loaded with varying views of reality regarding public issues. Our 24-hour media moguls carve out their audience, then broadcast a message custom-designed to hold the attention of these viewers or listeners. To do this, they tailor reality to the interests of the target audience. Providing the audience with reliable information becomes less important than getting them to watch and listen, again and again. The same is true for many political leaders or social interest groups who stake their future upon a view of reality narrow enough to confine the issues and sustain their voting constituency. Their message is not reality as it is, in all its fluid complexity, but reality as they wish it to be: simple and manageable. Believing in a fantasy rather than facing current issues truthfully obviates the need to continually research and reevaluate the facts, or to attempt to view the situation from diverse perspectives.

In the Oregon state legislature, I served with one legislator from a rural part of the state who had served several terms in office. His agenda encompassed a single subject: "No new taxes!" He kept his position interesting by resisting all new fees, contracts, or government spending of any kind. You had to admire the simplicity and clarity of his position. It was like a lullaby that allowed him to disengage from the complex realities of the budget process. His message of "No new taxes" may have gotten him reelected, but it also made him ineffective and kept him from dynamic involvement in the public conversation.

This kind but unproductive legislator always knew how he was going to vote, as did all his fellow legislators. He did not need to pay attention during committee hearings, floor debates, or caucus discussions. His unyielding commitment automatically excluded him from every negotiation and meaningful discussion, and prevented him from influencing others. By closing himself off from any modification of his position, he denied a basic reality: the world, and everyone in it, is an evolving, ever-changing, living organism. He remained blind to reality as it was.

Conscious public leaders seek to understand current reality in total, rather than focus only on the part of reality that supports our point of view. Business leaders call this a balanced score card. It is important to have a balanced score card to describe the upside and downside of current reality. Though a good leader may not have all the information he needs at the outset of a project, he is diligent in his researching, reading, listening, and learning to uncover the facts. If a business leader shares only the aspects of an issue that support her own narrow agenda, the downside is sure to be revealed later, resulting in lost opportunities. For this reason, making statements based on a limited view of reality breeds cynicism among our listeners, once they get the whole picture and discover what we omitted. Our society has become all too familiar with this limited way of communicating, or spinning, a message.

Learning to see reality as it is means viewing issues from an inclusive framework, one that allows for diverse perspectives. It means getting comfortable with not having all the answers. It means listening with an open mind to find out what is really going on. Strong-willed public leaders may have a habit of offering only their own point of view, assuming that whatever has worked in the past will surely work again. In the meantime, however, the world has changed. Leadership must transform to accommodate a chaotic new set of variables: the complexities of a global society. The new reality requires that public leaders keep an open playing field and a balanced score card.

Learning to Listen

Studies show that we spend 75 percent of our waking hours is verbal communication: 40 percent listening and 35 percent talking. Only 16 percent of our communication time is spent reading, and only nine percent writing. Politicians and public leaders are thrust into roles that require them to communicate verbally with much greater frequency and precision than is demanded of the average citizen. Our educational systems spend the majority of their time teaching reading and writing skills, however. The art of speaking and listening is taken for granted because we talk and listen to each other all day every day, right? But in fact, good listening does not come to us automatically. It's a misconception that the act of listening is instinctive. Deep, effective listening takes practice and awareness. It's important not to confuse listening with hearing. Hearing only exchanges facts. True listening is a potent force that builds trust and a sense of belonging. True listening empowers both the speaker and the listener.

How well do you listen? It may seem like a silly question, yet communications specialists tell us that Americans in general have lapsed into a lethargic habit of poor listening. It's no wonder: our TV, radio, and computers are all talking at us in a daily cacophony. As we spend increased time with electronic communication, we talk more and listen less. To become a great

It's a misconception that the act of listening is instinctive. Deep, effective listening takes practice and awareness.

listener, the first step is to realize that listening is an active, not a passive, process. Recognizing that listening is a distinct skill, professional coaching schools teach that there are *Three Levels of Listening*.

Level One is when you listen sporadically, sometimes tuning in and at other times tuning out what the speaker is saying. You are mainly paying attention to your own thoughts, considering what you want to say next. You follow the discussion only until you get a chance to speak. At this level of listening you may fake attention, nodding your head or saying, "mm-hmm," while preparing your response. For a politician, Level One listening is dangerous—you receive very little information this way, and you come off as phony or self-centered. If you are a politician you are often drawn into this level of listening because many people want your position on issues and you know you must respond well. An exchange of factual information is appropriate. However, listening in a way that focuses only on your own intended message, while treating the speaker's message as secondary (or worse, completely unimportant) prevents us from forging authentic connections with others.

In Level One listening you miss much of what is said, as well as what is between the lines. In this way, you limit your ability to adopt a perspective based on the facts. Your integrity is compromised because your information is incomplete.

If you consistently listen at Level One, you will be judged as self-centered and shallow, a typical politician who talks too much. When two leaders are listening to each other at this level, each one is thinking, "What's in it for me?" At this stage, communication breakdown is frequent, and the conversation lacks heart and meaning. No real exchange takes place. Very little collaboration or vision occurs at Level One.

Level Two listening focuses on what is being said, as well as what is not being said. You relinquish judgment so that you can hear someone else in a deep and meaningful way. Your attention is over there, with the person talking. You may respond with statements like, "Tell me more," or "How can we work together on this?" Powerful political conversations begin at this level, in which working together and building alliances becomes easier. The journey away from self-centeredness begins at Level Two. For conscious public leaders, the goal is to listen even more deeply, at Level Three.

Level Three listening is expansive, generous, and intuitive. You step back from the details of the moment in order to see and feel the larger context of the conversation. You listen deeply to the speaker, without allowing yourself to be distracted by his body language. You spontaneously respond appropriately and authentically. In Level Three listening, you remain aware of your own intuitive sense of what is being said; you listen to your spiritual center even as you respectfully listen to another. At Level Three listening, all games and political maneuvering stop. You enjoy the ease and naturalness of suspending your own thoughts while responding empathetically and authentically to another. For conscious public leaders, Level Three is our natural state of listening, where collaboration, political vision and inspiration thrive.

> At Level Three listening, all games and political maneuvering stop. You respond empathetically and authentically.

The Art of Asking Questions
and Living in Possibility

When I was 19, my college literature professor tried to convince me that the questions we ask in life are more important than the answers. The wisdom of this statement was lost on me at the time. In fact, historians are fond of saying that our current leaders will be evaluated in the future by the quality of the questions they pose today, rather than by the perceived problems they attempted to solve. What good does it do to solve a problem if the solution (and the problem) will soon be irrelevant?

Much of the Politics of Hope is about listening for possibility, resisting the urge to confine our perspective within predetermined notions. Conscious public leaders are skilled at asking a question purely for the sake of exploration and discovery, then listening intently. Our next question is born from the information we have just received, rather than from a set of preconceived notions we carry at the ready. Conscious public leaders, practitioners of the Politics of Hope, eschew rigid thinking. We know that rigidity—making up one's mind about anything and being unwilling to change it—is the enemy of fresh ideas. We know that creative collaboration emerges naturally in an environment of respectful listening. The fast pace of our global society presents new situations that could not have been conceived of only a few years ago. Einstein's often-quoted statement has never been more appropriate: "We can't solve problems by using the same kind of thinking we used when we created them."

> What good does it do to solve a problem if the solution (and the problem) will soon be irrelevant?

As a young teenager, I was fitted for eyeglasses. I remember well my first bespectacled drive home through the countryside. I asked my parents, "Have those trees always been there?" My new glasses had given me new sights; I was now able to see fine details as well as a broader perspective, which my limited vision had caused me to miss before. In the uncertain world of ideas and public policy, public leaders must constantly seek ways to expand and refine our vision. Asking probing, insightful questions and, most importantly, listening deeply for the answers, can reveal fresh aspects of an issue that we might have missed had we relied only on our own perception. One way to do this is to consider the question "What else might be happening here?" or "What else could this mean?" Suspending assumptions and truly listening for new possibilities is essential to the Politics of Hope. Though a creative stance often ignites further questions, it also offers greater possibilities. In order to live in possibility, we must give up our attachment to certainty. We must become willing to be surprised.

> What is it that I *don't know* that I don't know?

Conscious public leaders are willing to say, "I don't know the answer." We find freedom in saying, "I don't know." However, we can't stop there. We must go deeper, asking, "What is it that I *don't know* that I don't know?" For example, I know that I don't know much about nuclear biology or chemical engineering. I can freely and readily say, "I don't know," when it comes to those subjects. In this case, I *know* that I don't know. But there are surely things I'm ignorant about, knowledge that it may never have occurred to me that I might need and in which I'm lacking. So what is it that I *don't know* that I don't know?

We can ponder, discuss, question, research, and learn regarding the answers we don't know. In this way, we can fill in those gaps. But how can we open up to valuable knowledge in areas where we don't know we're lacking? This kind of inquiry is part of living in the mystery, which I'll go into in more detail in the next chapter. For now, it's enough to notice that our integrity is supported by humility: understanding that we don't even know all that we don't know! The public readily accepts those of us who embrace the complex world of not-knowing. It rejects leaders who make up answers and insist on living in a manageable fantasy.

If Everyone is Right, Who Will be Left? (Relinquishing the Notion that Others are Right or Wrong)

In Stage Two Traditional politics, success is measured by making others wrong and defeating them. It's a model that hearkens back to early civilization, when rulers gained power by acquiring more land, more slaves, more animals, and more products than their neighbors, usually by conquering them in battle. Dominating others, making them wrong, assuring that your opponents had less than you had—all these increased your chances of survival and success. It sounds archaic, even barbaric. But in fact our competitive society is still largely focused on defeating others. To succeed in life is to get ahead, meaning that someone—probably a lot of someones—must be left behind.

I am as competitive as anyone. I love sports, for instance. My heart pounds in the bottom of the ninth, with two outs and the bases loaded. I'm on my knees in the living room waiting with measured breath for the next fateful pitch. When I was in the retail business, I felt passionately that my products were the best and did all that I could to promote sales and beat out the competition.

Getting past the right-wrong model doesn't mean we eliminate the spirit of competition altogether. That isn't going to happen in any case. The goal is to honor our opponents, really listen to their ideas, consider what they have to offer, and look for ways to work together. If we listen only to those with whom we agree, we'll have only half the information we need to make wise decisions. Simply put, the two-party system works against the principle of teamwork. Fortunately, successful organizations and businesses have begun to cultivate an open-minded atmosphere in which a wide range of ideas and a spirit of collaboration can flourish. In political life, however, the dominate-or-die model keeps us from working together. Today's party leaders apparently don't believe the majority of citizens understand the concepts of interdependence and collaboration. Our political leaders may fear they'll seem weak if they advocate cooperation and respect. On the contrary, however, such a stance requires a lion's share of courage.

Leaders with integrity don't blame others, and we don't make excuses; we take responsibility for our actions. Consciously or subconsciously, it is a powerful human tendency to find fault with others rather than examine how our own actions may have contributed to our current difficulties. Learning to listen deeply in anticipation of endless possibilities, to see reality as it really is, and to take responsibility without making others wrong—these are not simply skills but ways of being. Living this way, conscious public leaders make friends with the truth: the basis of real integrity.

Trust: What Everyone Wants

Countless public opinion surveys and political polls tell this truth about trust: it is what citizens would most like to feel toward their public leaders. Time and again we hear, "Even if I don't agree with a politician, I would support him if I felt I could trust him." So what is trust anyway, and how do leaders earn it? There are two essential elements necessary to gain the trust of others: motives and the ability to follow through.

Our motives are closely related to our intentions (see chapter 8,

"Serving with Higher Motives"). Whether we operate from the highest motives or not, citizens must believe that their leaders' motives are pure. Once that threshold is crossed, the bond is sealed and trust begins. Erik Erickson's foundational stages of human development begin with the foundational stage of trust. Erickson knew that without trust, all other stages of human growth are impeded.

When we feel positive about another's motives, we believe what she says. We assume her intentions are good. However, if we suspect she is operating with ulterior motives, from a hidden or selfish agenda, saying one thing but doing the opposite, we feel manipulated by the partial disclosure on her part. We doubt her motives and we doubt her integrity.

Our skill and ability to follow through on commitments and agreements determines our trustworthiness. We regard another's ability to keep agreements positively when we observe that what she says is in alignment with what she does. I have worked with many well-meaning people who considered themselves strong and trustworthy leaders, but whose actions told a different story. Though their stated intentions were good, they lacked the willingness to squarely view current reality, to assess a situation with equanimity, to make plans to address what needed attention, and then to follow through. Though I may trust a leader's motives to be pure, if I can see that he currently lacks the ability to follow through, my trust in him remains guarded, incomplete.

> There are two essential elements necessary to gain the trust of others: motives and the ability to follow through.

Trust exists when we feel positive about someone's motives and capability. When we are engaged in trusting relationships, there is a sense of freedom. We know that any agreements we make are solid and will be fulfilled. We relax, trusting that if conditions change in some unexpected way, if the other must alter the original plan, she will honestly and in a timely way communicate the reason for her actions. Such trust naturally leads to collaborative and co-creative relationships.

Conscious public leaders enjoy discussing all the information at their disposal with the public. We don't feel afraid or tempted to hide uncomfortable facts; instead, we welcome the occasion to examine the facts to learn together, to discover new possibilities. Just as a termite can eventually bring down the mighty beams of a grand building, withholding information and presenting only part of the current reality can erode the foundation of trust that a public leader works hard to maintain among her supporters.

Stage Three Political Resignation has its origins in the frustration that follows a loss of trust. Having reluctantly given up on the dream of democracy, the Politically Resigned now grieve the fact that they no longer trust in public, corporate, or religious leaders. As Erickson pointed out, this lack of trust prevents humanity from creating the subsequent stages of community, collaboration, and commitment. At this writing, vast numbers of our citizens are stuck in this state of distrust.

I believe that constituents are forgiving, even generously forgiving, of human mistakes. But when a recurring pattern evolves—of half-truths and partial realities presented as truths—trust and forgiveness begin to erode. To revive the dream of democracy we must rebuild that trust, placing our hope in ourselves and in our conscious public leaders who hold the public's trust as a sacred gift.

We are entering a pivotal time in the history of our country and the world. Conscious public leaders know that to renew our political system, a great number of us must embody and model for our children the qualities of integrity and trustworthiness.

Coaching Exercise

Tell the Truth for Just 24 Hours!

Are you willing to accept a difficult challenge? Tell the truth, the complete truth and nothing but the truth for one whole day! Are you ready for the challenge? Here are the rules:

Select a day ahead of time. When you awaken on that day, be aware that this is the day on which you will be completely truthful until you go to bed. Make a solemn commitment to yourself to speak the complete truth without exception. If you are late for an appointment, no little white lies and no excuses. Just state the facts. Tell the truth. If you notice moments when you are prone to stretching the truth, notice the circumstances. What fears were underneath your desire to tell a lie?

Carry a notebook with you throughout the day and record even the slightest tendency to lie. (Call it what it is. If you aren't telling the truth, you're lying.) At the end of the day, look back and reflect on the times you were tempted to lie. In what circumstances did you most want to be untruthful? How did you feel when you told the truth in situations when you would normally tell a small lie? Did you notice more self-integrity when you told the truth? Was there an added sense of empowerment?

This exercise is often more difficult than expected, but the insights are enduring provided you are truthful with yourself. Remember that being truthful with yourself means that you will naturally be truthful with others.

12

Trusting the Mystery

We are born in mystery, we live in mystery and we die in mystery.

—Huston Smith, Ph.D.

Conscious public leaders have the capacity to lead in the realm of the unknown. We know how to move forward decisively even when the outcome of our efforts remains uncertain. As leaders, we accomplish this feat by trusting the creative process, which allows us to press on with faith and courage, even when the specific solution or conclusion we hope for is not yet fully visible. Our language, actions, and motives allow for and freely embrace the unknown aspects of our mission as leaders.

The challenge of living with ambiguity is not a new phenomenon, but it is an essential practice for 21st-century visionaries who seek to serve in a world beleaguered by increasing complexity and chaos. Threatened by uncertainty, many citizens would prefer to forgo all mystery, longing for the good old days when the rules were clear and life was simpler, if not easier. Even the most conscious of public leaders may wish the world were less complex and that the difficulties of human life were easier to navigate. Nevertheless, we do not allow our nostalgia to stymie reasonable attempts to move forward with creativity and courage into the uncertain future. Only citizens and public leaders who have accepted the challenge of finding inner order amidst outer chaos will have the capacity to lead. It's a new paradigm: By actively engaging in the creative process of shared leadership, conscious public leaders also share in a collective vision of fresh possibilities for the future. This creative process is the heart of collaboration. Wise citizens and public leaders consciously turn our attention to the creation of new working systems and relationships, rather than to the destruction of those with opposing views; thus, we have the ability to transform our culture of governance and revive democracy.

Learning to live with ambiguity, therefore, means that as leaders we consistently move our focus away from problem solving per se, and refocus on how to sustain a balanced life for all of the world's inhabitants. It is tempting to see problems as the exclusive province of our work, since problems exert painful pressure on our daily lives. Reacting to immediate problems, however, keeps our attention and our energies trained on what we don't want, and prevents us from embracing the creative process that would ultimately enable us to discover and accomplish what we do want.

The Problem with Problem-Solving

Leading from a problem-solving mentality is like trying to drive a car while looking in the rearview mirror. Looking backward at the problems of the past doesn't give us the clearest or most expansive view of where we are headed. It's wise to learn from our mistakes, of course. But when we place our primary energy on defining and solving problems, leaders ultimately get stuck in reaction mode. At first there may be a sense of accomplishment: a plan is generated and action begins to address the problem. Taking action is reassuring and it encourages voters. We're not like those other do-nothing leaders—we're doing something! Eventually, though, focusing on problems burns us out. Our original vision, the reason for our service, and our sense of positive possibilities all become atrophied.

When we focus on problems, our energy is directed toward what we *don't* want (the problem) rather than on what we *do* want. Our vision, like our goal, is limited to getting rid of an irritant, rather than focused on creating something delightfully effective or even artful. The more energy we place on solving problems, the more control problems in general will exert over our lives. The parameters of the problem begin to define every conversation. It is an insidious trap, but the problem focus keeps us mentally confined to very close quarters.

Whether we're attempting to apply public policy in a government agency, or allay the concerns of a particular community group, problem solving perpetuates a state of continuous oscillation. We attack the problem and for a while things seem to get better. We relax and forget about the issue. We experience relief and enjoy the illusion of progress. Later, however, when the same concern reappears, we're reminded that our solution did not confront the heart of the issue. This oscillation, the back-and-forth motion created by an attack/avoidance approach, masks our ability to create a larger vision, and we stay mired in a problem mentality.

> When we focus on problems our energy is directed toward what we *don't* want (the problem) rather than on what we *do* want.

Becoming expert problem solvers gives us a false sense of creativity and effectiveness. Focusing on problems is common among public leaders because it is the quickest way to alleviate pain. However, short-term thinking can never revive the real dream. The founders of our maverick form of government assumed a decidedly creative stance. Aware of problems but not blinded by them, they moved forward into the unknown territory of democracy. Taking persistent action toward a long-term beneficial outcome, rather than settling for piecemeal solutions in the short term, is the hallmark of a conscious public leader.

Focusing on problems has a dangerous by-product: it's addictive. We begin to seek the feeling of importance, the immediate gratification, of tackling some difficulty and keeping it at bay. In time, we may actually begin creating chaos, whether consciously or subconsciously, just to give ourselves an opportunity to feel important. Have you ever felt that things were going great in your life and then suddenly wondered, "When is the other shoe going to drop?" Those of us addicted to problem solving feel uncomfortable when things are going well. We like problems because they keep us focused on an attainable goal. They remove our discomfort about the unknown future. Conscious public leaders, on the other hand enjoy the process of creating a new vision for the future, however uncertain it may seem in present time. Because we're constantly working in service of our highest motives, we naturally feel good about ourselves. We don't need a crisis to attack in order to feel competent. Conscious public leaders know that there's always room for improvement, but we have no trouble accepting life when things are good.

> Taking persistent action toward a long-term beneficial outcome, rather than settling for piecemeal solutions in the short term, is the hallmark of a conscious public leader.

Public leaders who view life through the problem lens conjure up crises so they can ride in on their white horses and save the day. Most campaign themes boil down to "Elect me and I'll save you from impending disaster." Many social activists prone to this trend focus on cultural defects rather than on what is good and promising about America. For many, problems appear to give life meaning. But to become the authors of our democracy's destiny, we must take a broader view.

Make no mistake: our lives and businesses do encounter problems. As conscious public leaders we approach problems in service to our inspired vision. Not satisfied simply to arrive at an immediate solution, however, Stage Four leaders see problems as opportunities. We identify and solve a problem knowing that it helps to make way for a greater future dream. New energy is freed once the problem is removed, so life can be lived in closer accord with the highest motives of generosity, cooperation, and simple kindness. Resources are allocated and a new direction is set. When problems are addressed thus, always consciously moving toward the greater good, a spiral affect takes place that furthers the evolution of humanity as a whole.

To be comfortable with mystery, we must be in contact with our spiritual center. We must know the deepest inner core of who we are. Living in cooperative alliance with life's mystery in the form of our own inner spirituality gives birth to a state of perpetual creativity. As we unearth our passion for what we want to create, we begin to see our problems as way stations on the path that is moving us ever closer to an authentic life. Once we learn to accept the mystery of this constantly unfolding process, we discover that we're instinctively creative. We create as a matter of course. Best of all, we no longer need crises to help us feel we're accomplishing something. Exercising our creative and collaborative abilities gives life richness and meaning.

The Creative Process

The paradox of the creative process is that it is a *process* and *not* a formula. Just as there is no certain formula for creating a timeless work of art, there is also no single, surefire formula for coming to know your spiritual center, or even for being a good neighbor. The creative inspiration comes from within each of us individually, in its own time and in its own way, and that is the magical difference.

For an aspiring conscious public leader, embracing the creative process is essential to developing the capacity to lead in the realm of the unknown. Rather than offering a paint-by-numbers procedure guaranteeing a predictable outcome, embracing creativity means that each new step allows an opening for whatever is next. To continue in this way, a leader must engage fully in the matter at hand and trust in the unfolding process. Such an approach requires surrender, and it requires that we become detached from the outcome; we release our desire to stay in control. The creative process forms the basis of our democracy's imminent transformation to an age of collaborative leadership. As leaders who master the merging of creativity with the collaboration of the many, we will find ourselves at the forefront of cultural change in the 21st century.

Those who continue in a problem-focused vein, on the other hand, will miss the passion that is part and parcel of the creative process. They will be limited merely to responding to what is, rather than to what might be. Conscious public leaders able to lead amid the discomforts of not-knowing will be those who seek to honor the creative process of collaboration rather than to gratify the needs of the ego. The creative, collaborative process is not designed to bring the leader praise or keep her happy. The focus is on the process, not on the leader.

The following is a brief outline of the steps in the creative process. For a more thorough discussion, I recommend Robert Fritz's *Creating*. Fritz's brilliant insights have set a standard in both the arts and the business world for anyone seeking to wholeheartedly embrace the mystery of the creative process.

Start with a blank piece of paper. ***What do you really love?*** Answering this question is the first step in the creative process. What matters to you? What do you think about, dream about? Do you want to be a painter? Public speaker? Gardener? The more specific your answer the more focused you become, and the greater your rate of creative success. What you focus on is what you will create.

Fritz states that many people confuse problem solving with what they really want. For example when asked, "What do you want?" a leader may respond, "I want to help children." Why do children need helping? "Because so many children are unloved."

This public leader is trying to solve the problem of unloved children in the world, but by reaching to the pain of unloved children he has become frozen in a problem orientation. Instead, by remaining in the idea stage of the creative process and staying away from any effort to arrive at a specific solution, she could make the necessary room to explore what she really wants. At this stage, move from the general to the specific in defining what you want but avoid setting policies or any specific action. Visualize the ideal scenario, then write down words that paint the picture of what you love on this blank piece of paper. Just for now, stop trying to fix anything or anyone, and do this simply for the joy of imagining what would make your life more wonderful. This isn't about getting selfish; it's about getting self-knowledge.

If you are a public leader and want to work on behalf of children, do so simply because you love children. Acknowledge your love in this first stage, so the unfolding of your creative process reveals what outcomes you want to work toward, rather than focusing on the problems you want to eradicate.

Vision. Vision is the second stage of the creative process. It focuses on your desired result. If you stated in the first step, "I love gardening," your vision might be a garden in full bloom. Is the garden filled with flowers or vegetables? Create specific images that express your vision. At this point, you're likely to encounter an internal voice that comes up with reasons why your garden won't work. ("We live in a dry climate." "My yard is too small." "My husband won't help me till the ground.") Tell that voice to be silent for now, or simply ignore it. Paint the biggest and boldest vision possible. No nay-saying allowed!

For the public leader who loves children, the vision may be that all children have neighborhood playgrounds. The specific vision is coming to life now, with details and a specific picture. Continue to avoid critical judgments, ignore any reasons why it may not happen, and refine your vision.

Describe current reality in relationship to the results you want. This is where the rubber meets the road. What is actually going on? What currently supports your vision? What does not support your vision? Make two lists. Leadership consultant David Womeldorff, author of *Creating Sustainable Change: Seven Agreements for Accelerating Collaboration* states that an assessment of current reality must be honest and objective. We must see reality as it is, not as we wish it to be.

> It is when speaking your vision, giving words to it and painting a specific picture in your mind, that others become attracted to creating the same vision.

In fact, distorting reality (by denying, minimizing, or explaining away certain details) thwarts the creative process. Current reality is almost always a mixed message, Womeldorff writes. There is always something going on that supports or reinforces our capacity to manifest our vision, as well as circumstances that inhibit or challenge our ability to create the desired outcome. Making realistic lists of both obstacles and supporting factors in current reality allows us to take reasonable action.

Take action. This is the step that throws so many leaders into creative paralysis. Unsure how to begin, we wait for perfect conditions and guaranteed success. We tell ourselves that pondering, waiting, and further planning will help us control the outcome, or at least increase chances of success. Dreamers dream and planners plan. Conscious public leaders know how to dream *and* plan toward a specific vision. We also know how to take action to implement our dreams and plans when the time comes. We do not allow ourselves to be immobilized by perfectionism. Such leaders know that the first rule of action is "Always go to your strengths." Look at your list of current circumstances that supports your vision. This is the place to begin taking action. Enlist those who support your vision and take one step. Just do it!

The citizen who loves children and wants each child to have a playground must honestly assess the list of factors supporting her vision, and those opposing her vision, according to current reality. The list may include the names of community leaders who share the vision or the location of one piece of land already donated for the first new playground. Here is the genius in this step of the creative process: You begin to speak about your vision. It is when speaking your vision, giving words to it and painting a specific picture in your mind, that others become attracted to creating the same vision. Action begets action and forward motion begins. This step means taking action that supports your vision and moves toward creating the results you want. Too many leaders become distracted by the problems they see on the way. Bogged down by difficulties, they hesitate, either refusing to take decisive action or continuing to focus on potential problems, soon forgetting the vision that got them excited in the first place.

Learn and Evaluate. The creative process is a dynamic unfolding, a continual state of learning, adjusting, and responding to new information. Taking action and receiving feedback allows us to learn what's working and what isn't. Viewed in this light, obstacles and mistakes become learning opportunities. Conscious public leaders learn to work with the dynamic tension inherent in the creative process so that it actually drives further inspiration and feeds our vision. Rather than become discouraged, conscious public leaders use the very friction created by obstacles and challenges to define the path to our vision.

As great leaders, we do not hesitate to alter paths according to the learning we receive from the actions we take. We know the collaborative process makes new information available in service to the desired outcome. Brainstorming or trial-and-error methods, however, do not constitute action taken unless they are fully focused on creating the vision. Many a worthy public project has been side-tracked when the leaders involved could not keep their group focused on the desired result. Collaborative facilitation takes practice. As successful conscious public leaders of the future, we will know how to manage this process, always learning, adjusting, and evaluating our actions in service of the vision.

Build Momentum. This is my favorite step. It's where the fun begins! Here, everyone involved can feel the energy and the forward action toward a common goal. Energy invites further action, heightened learning, and positive movement toward the final result. Everyone can see and feel the success.

Without momentum, you may be faced with starting all over again. Successful public leaders have "creative antennae." They have learned the art of sensing momentum and know when to act on that momentum so as to attract others to the vision and begin moving forward. In this step, energy flows with grace and ease among all those involved. No one talks of burnout or frustration. The end result is at hand.

Know Your Next Step. This phase of the creative process allows the momentum to continue. To keep up the momentum toward realizing a goal, those involved must get a glimpse of what's coming up next. Successful leaders are always asking, "What's next?" The momentum continues if they are able to confidently meet each successive step, one after the next.

Completion. The ultimate joy of the creative process is, of course, to bring your creation into being. This stage can be difficult for some because it means that the project is over. The excitement and creative energy we had focused in the early stages is now gone. Highly creative people often enjoy the creative process more than they enjoy the final product. Others do not relish the final details required to wrap up a project and may resist the slower pace of finishing. Some avoid bringing any creation to completion in order to avoid evaluating whether the project was worthy of their efforts.

In the coaching profession we speak about "declaration of completion" and the power that such a declaration releases for new visions to emerge. By stating, "I am complete with this project," one experiences a sense of accomplishment and finality. A statement of completion also prevents endless tinkering with the creation. It allows us to see and accept that our project is done. The acknowledgment or declaration of the completion actually allows for the opening of new energy. Vigor is renewed and the creation process begins again.

Problem Solving or Creating: Which Path?

The essential question to ask as we consider which path to take in a given situation is this: "What is the pattern of results we want to create?" If we want to maintain the status quo and act according to a model built on the past, then focusing on problem solving is the best course of action. On the other hand, if we want something new, if we're seeking to adapt to change, to respond well in new environments, then we must adopt the creating model.

We may achieve episodic, short-term change with problem solving, but our short-term success will eventually undermine our vision, tricking us into believing that progress been made. For this reason, many efforts at positive change fail to produce the intended long-term results.

The key to embracing the mystery and chaos of our times is to commit to becoming a lifelong learner, skilled in the art of the creative, collaborative process. I love unraveling the rich web that mystery weaves throughout my life. I've even given a name to this process: "Donna's Treasure Hunt." Unanticipated treasures are secreted away all along my life's path. My vision is to unearth them, to hold them up to the light. The treasures exist—there's no doubt about that. My choices in life help me to discover them as I go, as I take this path or that, turning to correct my course when needed, listening to my traveling companions, and choosing my next possible step. It is one of the great paradoxes of conscious public leadership that following the mystery, the unknown, leads to the treasure. I may choose to struggle or feel discouraged at times, or I may choose to remain hopeful and confident. It's my choice. But the path is more joyous and more fruitful when I choose hope.

Coaching Questions

1. If you could generate any particular outcome as a public leader—regardless of whether you currently know how to accomplish it or whether you think it is "possible"—what would it be? Start with a blank piece of paper and follow the creative steps to write your vision.
2. What can you do in the next 30 days to begin making your vision a reality? Just take one step and begin.
3. Think of a situation or problem about which you feel anxious or fearful. What might you create (that currently does not exist) in order to solve that problem or eliminate that situation? (Asking this kind of question facilitates the shift from merely reacting against a problem to focusing on the desired outcome.)

13

Answering the Call

Mindfulness must be engaged. Once there is seeing, there must be acting. Otherwise what is the use of seeing?

—Thich Nhat Hanh

The six Essential Practices have taken you inward, preparing you for public leadership in the outer world. You are now ready for the Seventh Practice: Answering the Call.

The first six Essential Practices for becoming a conscious public leader encourage you to find your spiritual center, begin leading from higher motives, share and cultivate your unique gifts, develop integrity and trustworthiness, and embrace the process. Responding to the first six practices requires that you listen to the internal call: you must do the personal interior work that readies you for action in the world. Declaring your purpose and clarifying your calling are a result of this inner exploration. The Seventh Practice requires listening to the external call and turning *someday* into *now*.

If, as a civilized culture, we are to have public leaders who understand these transformative times, we must be willing to answer the call. Ours is an age that requires a shift away from the old style of leadership that has dominated humankind for much of our history. For simplicity's sake, let's say there are two basic forms of public leadership: (1) heroic and (2) collaborative. The 21st-century conscious political leader will master the art of leading through collaboration and partnership, eschewing the now outmoded heroic style that encourages, even requires, dominion over others.

In heroic leadership, the objective is always clear: to win the game (or battle) and dominate others, as is the case with the two-party political system. A plan to overthrow the enemy is developed and the heroic leader undertakes to execute the plan—the majority of heroic leaders are problem solvers rather than inventors or creators. The heroic leader states his direction and convinces others of its rightness, often with contagious passion and enthusiasm. Followers may be inspired by the heroic leader's charismatic certainty. His unwavering vision comforts followers who have not experienced the power and freedom of the collaborative process. They may neglect to question the heroic leader's vision, strategies, or motives. Such followers often believe the myth that if one leader is unsuccessful, the organization need only locate a new hero who can erase their uncertainties with a new vision, thereby staving off chaos and saving the day. A single leader shows the way, solves the problems, and takes responsibility, credit, or blame for the outcomes that occur on his watch. By definition, then, organizations or cultures that operate according to the heroic leadership model disempower their constituents or members.

> Organizations or cultures that operate according to the heroic leadership model disempower their constituents or members.

In times of emergency such as the attack on the World Trade Center, September 11, 2001, an entire culture may resort to the idea that the heroic leader is their only hope. It isn't surprising, since this style of leadership is all that we have known in the past, and it is human nature to call upon what has worked in the past in times of crisis. How compelling it is to pin our hopes on the hero images that have been celebrated for centuries in our cultural stereotypes and storytelling! When we've been afraid in the past we tended to regress, wanting mainly to be comforted, to trust that our leaders were wiser and more informed, that they would take care of us. Now that we see the emperor's nakedness, however, we ourselves feel more vulnerable than ever. What to do?

Conscious public leaders, even in times of crisis, understand that leadership requires collaboration and partnership. Colin Powell, appointed Secretary of State by President George W. Bush, is a former military leader trained in traditional hierarchical forms of leadership. As a military leader in time of war and national emergency, he has made a successful career based upon collaboration. An article in *AARP* Magazine, "Behind Open Doors: Colin Powell's Seven Laws of Power," lists a few of Secretary Powell's key principles of leadership: (1) Get the real dirt, head for the trenches. The people in the field are closest to the problem, therefore that is where the real wisdom is. (2) Share the power. Powell says, "Plans don't accomplish the work. It is the people who get things done." (3) Powell adheres to two leadership premises: "People are competent and every job is important." (4) Never let your ego get so close to your position that when your position goes, your ego goes with it. Powell explains that too many leaders get so trapped in fixed ways of seeing things that they can't cope when the world changes.

Does this sound like a military man trained in traditional military thinking? Hardly. While you may or may not disagree with his politics, these principles of leadership are based upon the tenets of collaboration living inside the hierarchical military chain of command. This is breakthrough leadership emerging from a traditional top-down model. It is a significant shift for a military leader to list among his principles of leadership "Share the power." Colin Powell has discovered that including and empowering people is essential to the success of any enterprise. These insights can be of immense value to those tempted to believe that the old style of hierarchical, commander-in-chief thinking is the only way to lead.

In the world of sports we often assume that the heroic leadership model works best. After all, the coach knows the game better than his players do, and the team must listen to one voice, right? An interview with Phil Jackson, one of the most successful coaches in National Basketball Association history, reveals his understanding of the collaborative process within the team perspective this way: "We're all susceptible to falling down (and being dunked on) and being exposed. But when we lose our fear of that and look to each other, then vulnerability turns into strength, and we can take responsibility for our place in the larger context of the team and embrace a vision in which the group imperative takes precedence over personal glory." This is a coach who deals with the egos of multimillion-dollar sports superstars, but he has learned to juggle the paradox of independence and interdependence. In *Sacred Hoops,* Jackson writes, "Basketball is a sport that involves the subtle interweaving of players at full peak to the point where they are thinking and moving as one." So even in the sports world, where many believe the coach is duty-bound to act as a heroic leader, the new, successful coaches strike a delicate balance. They have learned to weave the unique gifts of each player into a beautifully choreographed winning team, successfully meshing individuality with interdependence.

In the public arena, the heroic leadership model is not only outdated but also creates an unrealistic expectation of political leaders. When we look to political leaders as saviors, we abdicate responsibility. We wait for them to tell us what to do. It's a scenario that creates improbable expectations of our leaders and weakens us as citizens. It keeps us from engaging in the social and political process essential to a true democracy. When public leaders fail to meet our unrealistic expectations, they are often blamed for having a meager vision or an inability to execute. The old model of leader-as-savior thus perpetuates the cycle of public cynicism: it encourages more and more citizens to drop out of the public discussion.

In the collaborative leadership model, we focus on the process rather than on the leader. The job of the collaborative leader is to ensure that the collaborative process is focused and leads to results by the many—it is not to impose our own will on the outcome and dominate others in doing so. The most important job of the collaborative leader is to be the keeper of the process.

The assumption that citizens should be informed and can make wise decisions is the very heart of democracy. If this assumption is rejected, believing in one heroic leader becomes the default. In the first half of the 20th century, American philosopher John Dewey articulated the original founders' vision of participatory democracy based upon two fundamental beliefs: the capacity of human beings to participate rationally and effectively in public life, and the desirability and practicality of their full participation. Dewey believed a person's capacity to participate could be nurtured in ways that supported informed political action.

Dewey's critics, in particular his contemporary Walter Lippmann, opposed this viewpoint. They believed that the judgment of ordinary people could not be trusted and that their participation in public life should therefore be limited. An intelligent, informed, and privileged group of people should govern on behalf of all, they asserted. This view is the prevailing assumption underlying Stage Two Traditional politics. If we are to restore the nobility of politics and public leaders, we must develop our capacity to teach the collaborative process so that the collective wisdom is supported by effective leadership. What is collaborative leadership, then? What are its results, and how do we learn it?

> In the collaborative leadership model, we focus on the process rather than on the leader.

Characteristics of Collaborative Leadership

In *Collaborative Leadership: How Citizens and Civic Leaders Can Make a Difference,* David Chrislip and Carl Larson write that the primary role of collaborative leaders is to promote and safeguard the process. Collaborative leaders are not rulers but facilitators. Here I have summarized the characteristics of the collaborative leader as facilitator into six essential roles.

1. Coach and facilitate; sustain inspiration and a belief that new methods can work.
2. Actively lead the process as a peer invested in the people by building trusting relationships and safeguarding the collaborative process.
3. Assure broad-based involvement and shared ownership of the process by all involved.
4. Create agreements among those involved that direct the process and promote interaction.
5. Practice patience and help participants understand the value of taking time to allow the process to take shape.
6. Model the collaborative process by actively practicing it in thinking, speech, and action.

These are a few of the keys to successful collaboration. The most fundamental of all the characteristics, however, is to include a broad base of stakeholders in the collaborative process. Great care must also be taken to ensure that the stakeholders bond together, that they share a common vision. Sufficient time and energy must be given so that participants may learn about one another. Informal outings, social gatherings, and programs specifically designed to build trusting relationships are essential in the early stages of the collaborative process. Those who are problem-oriented, who want things solved immediately, may criticize the time it takes to build relationships. They may resist making the effort to hear and appreciate the point of view of all group members. For this reason, it is essential to create opportunities for bonds to grow between members of any collaborative group, whether it be a governor's staff, corporate officers, or a nonprofit board of directors. The willingness to listen to each other is crucial to any successful collaboration.

Members of a collaborative group may come together around a problem or an urgent concern. The individuals often feel suspicious of one another and may suspect that the group won't be able to accomplish much. Due to our current cynicism and mistrust toward politicians, this is especially true of public issues directly involving elected officials. Acting as coach, however, the collaborative leader can make a difference. Investing people in the process and working to help the whole group accomplish their common vision becomes much more important than who is in charge. The collaborative leader keeps this focus, working behind the scenes to assure that everyone is heard, that a shared vision is reached which represents the whole.

> The collaborative leader focuses on serving others within the process of leading rather than focusing on himself.

This is the basis of Robert Greenleaf's seminal book, *Servant Leadership*. The collaborative leader focuses on serving others within the process of leading rather than focusing on himself. Such a leader understands that systems are only as good as the individuals who lead them. Greenleaf states:

> The future society may be just as mediocre as this one. It may be worse. And no amount of restructuring or changing the system or tearing it down in the hope that something better will grow will change this. There may be a better system than the one we

now know. It is hard to know. But, whatever it is, if
the people to lead it well are not there, a better system
will not produce a better society.

Today's public issues are so complex and changing so rapidly that
one person cannot possibly provide all the leadership skills necessary
to address every urgent concern. Thus, the collaborative process is
essential. In a true democracy, all our unique gifts and contributions
are needed, as we saw in chapter 9. True collaboration simply cannot
take place unless the many are involved, unless each person brings
his individual attitudes, perspectives, and talents to the table. This
new transformative leadership model will not be successful if only
the educated and elite are allowed to serve.

I witnessed the beauty of the collaborative process and the magic
of each person bringing their unique gifts to the process when I
worked for the Sisters of the Holy Names. As we have seen, in a
process that took nine years, the Sisters envisioned, planned,
designed, financed, built, marketed, and opened a successful
$90 million continuing care retirement center to serve their retired
sisters and the aging members of the surrounding communities. This
extraordinarily complex project involved creating a new health
care system, architectural plans, a construction team, and a team
of insurance and finance experts; assembling publicity and
communications specialists; providing social and spiritual direction;
locating consultants skilled in government permits; and creating
transportation teams and a management, marketing, and operations
team! The sisters assembled a dynamic group of professionals as they
grew this risky operation. The 16-member coordinating group (the
sisters often referred to their steering committee as their "rudder
committee," as though it were a rudder on a boat) was empowered to
make decisions, with the sisters ultimately in charge. Each member
knew that the sisters insisted on complete honesty, open communica-

tion, respect for other team members, and the involvement of all. The extra time it took to genuinely listen to everyone tested some people's patience and resolve. In the end, the project was hailed as a huge success by the sisters, their neighbors, and the retirement community residents. Even the investors who purchased the bonds to help build the community were repaid ahead of schedule.

What are the initiatives that successfully teach collaboration? If we consciously choose to move away from heroic leadership to collaborative leadership, how do we learn these successful techniques? Many new education and training models have taken shape in the last 10 years, among them The American Leadership Forum, nonprofit leadership training program located in several states and the publisher of Chrislip and Larson's *Collaborative Leadership*. This group has been training conscious public leaders in the collaboration model for over a decade. There are others championing the cause of collaboration, as well: Harrison Owen and his Open Space Technology has made significant contributions to a cease-fire in a 7-year conflict in the Niger Delta region of Africa. Dr. Don Beck's Spiral Dynamics model of leadership has been integral in altering the dominance of apartheid in South Africa and in transforming the political leadership there. Dr. Beck has made more than 65 trips to South Africa as a consultant and leadership trainer. By applying his transformative model of Spiral Dynamics, he has significantly contributed to new thinking in South Africa. In the same vein, my own work with the Politics of Hope at the Bainbridge Leadership Center is dedicated to teaching the collaborative model through political leadership coaching, seminars, and public education.

These new programs teach that one's own personal transformation comes first, so that we can make the necessary shift from the temptations of the heroic model to the success of the collaborative model. The payoff comes in lasting results that clearly demonstrate success.

The Success of the Collaborative Model

The success of the collaborative leadership philosophy refers to tangible results that lead to transformed public cultures, that create vision and momentum, that engender new hope that our democracy can adequately address issues that matter to people. I believe that collaborative leadership has the power to eventually create a world that works for us all—that it can successfully revive the dream of democracy.

Success within the collaborative model does not come without attention, sweat, focus, and yes, years of work. True collaboration requires an honest assessment of the desire for change (seeing current reality). Sometimes we speak of change when we really mean "Why doesn't everyone else agree with me?" This phenomenon emerges again and again in the two-party structure. Change is simply seen as changing the party in control. It doesn't refer to the significant change that would be sparked by true collaboration— in which all stakeholders sit at the table, genuinely listening for possibility, questioning assumptions, and building new alliances across old political boundaries. Many who cry out for change simply want to see someone new seated at the head of the table, someone who will act and lead according to the old heroic model. They resist a scenario that empowers all players, that offers a seat to the disenfranchised.

> True collaboration requires an honest assessment of the desire for change (seeing current reality).

Inviting and encouraging participation by all those seated at the table is essential to the success of collaboration. We don't begin with a list of names of the most powerful, wealthiest individuals. All stakeholders must have a seat. Diverse perspectives enhance the wisdom of the group and expand the possibilities for addressing a problem or concern. The collaborative process, therefore, begins with an accurate expression of reality reflected in the inclusion of all stakeholders. Without such inclusion of essential players, any outcome is destined to be flawed, ultimately renewing cynicism and stifling hope.

The collaborative model requires a shift from merely implementing a heroic leader's plan to working toward a collaborative vision. During the early stages of their work, the Sisters of the Holy Names did not tell their advisory group what to plan or how to plan it. They simply stated their desire to continue to live on their land and to create a project consistent with their values. Within those perameters, they invited people they trusted to join them, and then they engaged themselves fully in the planning and collaborative process. They believed that a broader team of people could help create something that they could not envision or accomplish by themselves. They did not know the outcome, yet they embraced the unknown with curiosity and a willingness to explore, to discover. Working with the sisters, I came to realize that this was faith: the trust that as yet unseen results will be born of mystery.

I have attempted to offer you a glimpse of the role of the collaborative leader. Marvelous books, case studies, and articles exist that examine the parts and practices of the collaborative process in much deeper detail. Having briefly outlined the characteristics of the two basic styles of leadership—collaborative and heroic—I hope I have made it clear that the collaborative model is best suited to conscious public leaders in the 21st century.

The Seven Essential Practices for becoming a conscious public leader begin with our inner work, in the deep spiritual center that lives within all; from there it moves to the outward expression of collaborative leadership. By trusting the collaborative process, we reap the dynamic energy of creative inspiration. It is the kind of energy from which all great human endeavors arise. By its nature, such energy gathers momentum. Before long, a mountain of evidence will have amassed, supporting what once was considered a radical idea: Hope is viable. As we engage in the inner and outer work of collaboration, as we persist in the creative process of shared leadership, we accomplish a human feat much greater than merely solving problems. We keep hope alive.

Coaching Questions

1. What aspects of collaborative leadership most readily appeal to you?
2. Think of at least one person in your life who exemplifies a collaborative leader. What admirable qualities does he or she possess? How might you incorporate those qualities into your own life?
3. To whom will you talk about your sense of calling? What information will you need to gather in order to determine your next steps? By applying the creative process, trusting the mystery, and having faith in yourself, you can turn someday into now.

14

Turn Someday Into Now

If there is anything you can do or dream you can, begin it. Boldness has genius, power and magic in it. Begin it now.

—Goethe

If you have read this far, you cannot avoid answering the call. As I said before, you picked up this book up for a reason. Something is stirring in you, as it is in me and in millions of other citizens. We believe in our country and want to make good use of the gifts that have been bestowed on us as citizens of the wealthiest and most powerful nation in the world's history. With those gifts comes the responsibility to rise above individual and personal interests and give back the kind of effort that will help all of us—all of humanity—to evolve into a higher awareness of our collective interdependence.

Political evolution depends upon our participation. We are a species gifted with insight into both our inner and outer conditions. Thus we may consciously choose our own direction. Our interdependence means that our survival rests on collaborative choices. We now face a crucial question: Must we experience tragedy and catastrophe in order to learn collaboration, or can we accelerate our own evolution by making conscious, creative choices? More and more scientific evidence is proving that the actions and consciousness of individuals affect the whole. Research into humankind's collective wisdom, or collective intelligence as it is also called, strongly suggests that individual choices and contributions are, in fact, essential to our collective progress as a species. People become conscious public leaders not because they tell others how to evolve, but because they take the first brave steps in an evolutionary direction, inviting others into the creative venture of shared leadership.

What Is Collective Intelligence?

We all have had this experience: In the midst of a gathering, we feel a potent and palpable energy in the room. It can happen in a work seminar, a church gathering, a weekend away with friends, a spiritual retreat, or a meeting at work. Suddenly something shifts, and the shared vision of everyone present clearly emerges. Along with this awareness comes the shared sense of a Higher Power: that the sum of us as a whole is greater than our individual parts. It's a feeling similar to that experienced by a sports team when suddenly everything jells and all the players are in the zone. The players perform with ease and grace, moving in harmony with their teammates. Watching it happen, the spectators also feel elated, inspired, transported to higher ground.

> We now face a crucial question: "Must we experience tragedy and catastrophe in order to learn collaboration, or can we accelerate our own evolution by making conscious, creative choices?

Collective intelligence, as it is often called, describes the phenomenon of the group mind and the accompanying flow of energy that seems spontaneously to elevate the individuals involved into an experience of the greater whole. We experience collective intelligence when we're with close friends, loved ones, business associates, or relatives and the same thought occurs to us at the exact same moment. Call it synergy, coincidence, or miracle.

Whatever it is, we all have such experiences. We're part of the whole of humanity, the whole of the inhabitants of our world.

What will spark a spontaneous awareness of collective intelligence? In my own experience, simply listening at Level Three (see chapter 11) guarantees that I will feel a shift in the energy and connection with the person speaking. This deep connection both sharpens our focus and expands our view of current circumstances. This shift of attention allows us to witness our interconnected group intelligence. All at once, we see the big picture. It is from this vantage point that we feel hopeful about the future.

I have been interested in the notion of collective intelligence for many years, first as a community mental health nurse and later in my personal studies of the mind/body connection. Although once considered a radical notion, it is now generally accepted that what we think affects our bodies. Now for the first time, scientists have begun to document the phenomenon of collective intelligence. We have far more power than we once imagined, either to make ourselves sick or to keep ourselves healthy. Three decades ago early studies demonstrated that people who prayed for others had an impact on their health. The researchers who made these findings were initially discounted as religious extremists. Now however, dozens of studies have shown that individuals who collectively pray for others promote the healing process of patients thousands of miles away!

The Institute of Noetic Sciences was founded by astronaut Edgar Mitchell. After his walk on the moon, Mitchell was overwhelmed by a powerful sense of the unity of all of creation. While attending a recent IONS annual conference, I heard Marilyn Schlitz, a scientist whose work is IONS-funded, report on her distance healing project. Schlitz has repeatedly demonstrated with verifiable data in over 150 scientific studies that individuals and groups can use visualization, relaxation, what she categorizes as a "healing force greater than themselves" to heal others, to a statistically significant degree. A small group of people acting collectively for good can have a decidedly positive impact in the world.

Collective intelligence is not science fiction. Scientific journals are publishing a growing number of articles providing strong evidence that we can create and develop work and living environments that promote collective consciousness. The question has changed from "Is collective intelligence real?" to "What conditions foster its emergence?" and "How can we as a culture nurture and enhance the experience (our political habitat)?" Most of all, how can our collective intelligence be directed toward the collective good?

If a collaborative leader brings stakeholders together to address a community concern and create a new vision, the science of collective intelligence says that the individuals "cross-pollinate." Their collective wisdom ensures that their endeavors are more likely to succeed. As for the Politics of Hope, our collective intelligence cannot expand and evolve without your participation. Knowing this, how can you not participate? If you choose to remain politically resigned, depressed, and disengaged, you cheat the whole of humanity. By withholding your gifts, you rob the collective intelligence of your contribution.

How can you not participate? If you choose to remain politically resigned, depressed, and disengaged, you cheat the whole of humanity. By withholding your gifts, you rob the collective intelligence of your contribution.

When, as public leaders we consciously choose the collaborative leadership model rather than the heroic model, we welcome all forms of contribution. We assume that everyone has something to offer the whole group. To revive the dream of real democracy, the masses—we the people—must participate in a way that both addresses urgent issues and cultivates our ongoing capacity to foster the common good. Animal and plant species that survive over millennia do so because they learn to adapt and work together in uncanny, often previously untried, ways. As citizens of a wealthy and powerful country, what will we do to ensure the survival of all humanity? Will we freely choose to work together, to welcome and shape the unknown on everyone's behalf? Will we learn to harness our collective wisdom to promote the public good? Will we choose a course of action based on hope?

The decision to consult our collective intelligence to accomplish political and cultural change naturally creates a shift in our understanding of our independence and our individual freedoms. Remember when I asked you to hold in one hand the idea of freedom and individuality, and to hold in the other hand the idea of the interconnectedness of all things? Weigh both concepts . . . balance them in your hands. You hold a paradox. This is a new kind of balance that we, as citizens, are just beginning to recognize. Gathering strength from the collective wisdom, we can accelerate our ability to hold this paradox and apply it to our governance. It will take all our shared talent and character, and no small amount of intellectual wherewithal. Understanding that we hold a responsibility to be entirely true to ourselves and also to choose actions that support our collective good is the key to making the next political evolutionary leap.

Organizations Making a Difference

Here in Seattle, Microsoft cofounder Paul Allen has invested millions of dollars in a brain research center. Throughout the world, scientists are predicting that brain research will become the next great arena of scientific discovery, unlocking the previously mystifying complexities of the brain and mind. Such research is bound to have an extraordinary impact on our lives and on our understanding of ourselves as human beings. Paul Allen's investment in brain research is just one example of powerful and influential people dedicating resources to help us learn more about the mind's influence on our individual and collective future.

Another group focusing on leadership and the collective intelligence is Washington State's Whidbey Institute. Their "Leadership for the New Commons" series focuses on cultivating leadership appropriate to a "radically interdependent world." In a recent newsletter, leadership consultant Larry Daloz recalls a conversation with a physician who was feeling overwhelmed by the complexity of our times. "If the world is so tangled, so much of a swamp, what can one person do that would possibly make any difference?" the doctor asked.

"That's just the point," interjected a young teacher who was listening in on their conversation. "If you really get interdependence in your bones, you realize that everything you do makes a difference. You *can't avoid* making a difference! Then it's a matter of aligning ourselves with the forces that are making a positive difference!"

Daloz writes of the exchange, "Paradoxically, it would seem, the very conditions that make us feel powerless can lead us through." Feeling powerless doesn't absolve us from action. Our sense of overwhelm can signal a need to stop and assess, to make room for the collective wisdom to emerge and create. We can begin consciously turning our energies toward this end.

Carol Frenier is project coordinator for the Fetzer Institute, a private foundation that has launched a research project to look at ways to encourage work environments that promote conversation and group wisdom. Frenier summarized the personal accounts of over 150 individuals who had experienced moments of collective wisdom. She reports that the majority of those who experienced this emergence feel that the purpose of this wisdom is to "midwife a new social/spiritual order of an evolutionary magnitude . . . one that is already emerging of its own power." As we revive the dream of democracy, our collective wisdom demands that we evolve in a direction which will best ensure the survival of our species. The Politics of Hope is as practical and essential as that.

Other business leaders, such as Joseph Jaworski, founder of the American Leadership Forum, which teaches collaborative leadership, understand the evolutionary leap we are about to make. He and his partner, Peter Senge, the business guru who transformed the business world in 1990 with his book *The Fifth Discipline,* have joined forces to accelerate the evolutionary leap, creating a worldwide conversation between leaders who are ready to make a radical shift in order to meet our shared global challenges. Their Global Leadership Initiative is focused on helping us reach the tipping point. Not only accepting and planning for but also acting in concert with the changes inherent in our rapidly changing current reality, these pioneers epitomize the Stage Four conscious public leader. They refuse to be stopped by the fear that arises when they consider the long list of world concerns—global warming, the wide gap between the haves and have-nots, world hunger, war

> Our collective wisdom demands that we evolve in a direction which will best ensure the survival of our species. The Politics of Hope is as practical and essential as that.

and terrorism, and on and on—the issues that might herald the annihilation of humankind. They understand that their individual actions can accelerate the collective wisdom and inspire others (you and me) to break through to new stages of leadership. These examples of leadership, research, and teaching feed the dream of real democracy. They illustrate our move from Stage Three Political

Resignation to the Politics of Hope. Your decision to become a conscious public leader is evidence of our evolutionary unfolding toward a world culture that reveres the common good. We're on our way to the tipping point!

Your role is vital. Without your participation, your wisdom, there will be a hole in our collective intelligence; the outcome of our shared efforts will be incomplete. To evolve to a higher order of life, we must all be involved. This is the law of evolution and the law of collective intelligence.

Margaret Mead said, "Never underestimate the power of a small group of committed people to change the world. In fact, it is the only thing that ever has." Her statement is a testimony to the potency of our collective intelligence. A small group of individuals can change the world because what begins with a few committed individuals sharing their gifts and speaking their wisdom builds a momentum of cross-pollination and expansion. Visions jell, and a Higher Power is brought to bear that stirs up creative action. All good and evolved ideas find their time, their tipping point. I challenge you to contemplate this phenomenon and find your role in it.

My coaching education, my professional philosophy, and my heart of hearts encourage me constantly to challenge my clients. I urge you also to let your vision be grander, to stretch your vision so that you take in the world in new ways. It is my role as a political leadership coach to challenge assumptions, to nudge others forward, to encourage them to see what they don't know that they don't know that they don't know. Our next evolutionary leap depends on you. Your conscious decision to contribute to our collective wisdom cannot wait until you are completely ready, until you have a perfect plan. *Someday* is the day that never comes. Don't wait for someday, or the right day. The time to take the next step is just before you think you're ready. "Boldness has genius, power and magic in it," said Goethe. Turn someday into now.

Beck, Don. *Spiral Dynamics: Mastering Values, Leadership, and Change*. Malden, Mass.: Blackwell Publishers, 1996.

Bennis, Warren. *On Becoming a Leader*. Reading, Mass.: Perseus Books, 1994.

Berry, Wendell. *Citizenship Papers*. Washington, D.C.: Shoemaker and Hoard, 2003.

Bohm, David. *On Dialogue*. New York: Routledge, 1996.

Bolman, Lee, and Terrence Deal. *Leading With Soul: An Uncommon Journey of Spirit*. San Francisco: Jossey-Bass, 2001.

Bridges, William. *Transitions: Making Sense of Life's Changes*. Boulder, Colo.: Perseus Books, 1980.

Brodie, Fawn. *Thomas Jefferson: An Intimate History*. New York: Norton Books, 1974.

Brown, Dan. *The Da Vinci Code*. New York: Doubleday Publishing, 2003.

Chrislip, David, and Carl Larson. *Collaborative Leadership: How Citizens and Civic Leaders Can Make a Difference*. San Francisco: Jossey-Bass, 1996.

Collins, James, and Jerry Porras. *Built to Last: Successful Habits of Visionary Companies*. New York: Harper Business, 1994.

Cousins, Norman. *"In God We Trust": The Religious Beliefs and Ideas of the American Founding Fathers*. New York: Harper, 1958.

Covey, Stephen. *First Things First: To Live, to Love, to Learn, to Leave a Legacy*. New York: Simon & Schuster, 1994.

Daloz, Larry. "Everything Is Hitched to Everything." *Whidbey Institute Newsletter*, Spring 2004.

Davila, Florangela. "King's Daughter Rouses Audience." *Seattle Times*, Jan. 17, 2004.

Dionne, E. J. *Why Americans Hate Politics*. New York: Simon & Schuster, 1991.

Dyer, Wayne. *There's a Spiritual Solution to Every Problem*. New York: HarperCollins, 2002.

Eisler, Riane, and David Loye. *The Partnership Way: New Tools for Living & Learning*. San Francisco: HarperSanFrancisco, 1990.

Erickson, Erik. *Childhood and Society*. New York: W. W. Norton, 1986.

Ervin, Keith. "Friends' Fund-Raiser Softens Political Line." *Seattle Times,* September 4, 2003.

Eswaran, Eknath. *Gandhi, the Man: The Story of His Transformation*. New York: Nilgiri Press, 1997.

Fitzgerald, Catherine, and Jennifer Berger, eds. "Leadership and Complexity of Mind." *Executive Coaching: Practices and Perspectives*. Palo Alto, Calif.: Davies-Black, 2002.

Fox, Matthew. *The Reinvention of Work: A New Vision of Livelihood for Our Time*. San Francisco: HarperSanFrancisco, 1994.

Fritz, Robert. *Creating: A Practical Guide to the Creative Process*. New York: Ballantine Books, 1991.

Fritz, Robert. *The Path of Least Resistance: Principles for Creating What You Want to Create*. Walpole, N.H.: Stillpoint Publishing, 1984.

Fuller, R. Buckminster. *Critical Path*. New York: St. Martin's Press, 1981.

Gladwell, Malcolm. *The Tipping Point: How Little Things Can Make a Big Difference.* Boston: Little, Brown, 2000.

Glassner, Barry. *The Culture of Fear: Why Americans Are Afraid of the Wrong Things.* New York: Basic Books, 1999.

Greenleaf, Robert, *Servant Leadership,* New Jersey, Paulist Press, 1977

Hamilton, Craig. "Come Together: The Mystery of Collective Intelligence." *What Is Enlightenment?* Magazine, May-June 2004.

Hanh, Thich Nhat. *Living Buddha, Living Christ.* New York: Riverhead Books, 1997.

Harari, Oren. "Behind Open Doors." *AARP Magazine,* Jan.-Feb. 2002.

Harkins, Philip. *Powerful Conversations: How High-Impact Leaders Communicate.* New York: McGraw Hill, 1999.

Hendricks, Gay, and Kate Ludeman. *The Corporate Mystic: A Guidebook for Visionaries with Their Feet on the Ground.* New York: Bantam Books, 1997.

Hock, Dee. Birth of the Chaordic Age. San Francisco: Berrett-Koehler, 1999.

Hubbard, Barbara Marx. *Conscious Evolution: Awakening the Power of Our Social Potential.* Novato, Calif.: New World Library, 1998.

Hunter, James C. *The Servant: A Simple Story About the True Essence of Leadership.* Prima Lifestyles, 1998.

Jackson, Phil. *Hoop Dreams.* New York: Hyperion Press, 1995.

Kegan, Robert. *In Over Our Heads: The Mental Demands of Modern Life.* Cambridge: Harvard University Press, 1994.

Kegan, Robert, and Lisa Laskow Lahey. *How the Way We Talk Can Change the Way We Work: Seven Languages for Transformation.* San Francisco: Jossey-Bass, 2001.

Krisco, Kim. *Leadership and the Art of Conversation: Conversation as a Management Tool. Prima Lifestyles,* 1997.

Kubler-Ross, Elisabeth. *On Death and Dying.* New York: Scribner Publishing, 1997.

Levoy, Gregg. *Callings: Finding and Following an Authentic Life.* New York: Three Rivers Press, 1998.

Loeb, Paul. *Soul of a Citizen: Living With Conviction in a Cynical Time.* New York: St. Martin's Griffin, 1999.

Maslow, Abraham. *Psychology of Being.* Hoboken, NJ: John Wiley & Sons, 1968.

McCullough, David. *John Adams.* New York: Simon & Schuster, 2001.

Morgan, Edmund Sears. *The Birth of the Republic, 1763-89.* Chicago: University of Chicago Press, 1992.

Parks, Sharon Daloz. *Big Questions, Worthy Dreams: Mentoring Young Adults in Their Search for Meaning.* San Francisco: Jossey-Bass, 2000.

Patterson, Kerry. *Crucial Conversations: Tools for Talking When Stakes Are High.* New York: McGraw-Hill, 2002.

Peck, M. Scott. *The Different Drum: Community Making and Peace.* New York: Touchstone, 1988.

Peck, M. Scott. *The Road Less Traveled.* New York: Touchstone, 1988.

Putnam, Robert: *Bowling Alone: The Collapse and Revival of American Community.* New York: Touchstone, 2001.

Ray, Paul, and Sherry Ruth Anderson. *Cultural Creatives: How 50 Million People Are Changing the World.* New York: Harmony Books, 2000.

Ritter, Kurt, and Martin Medhurst, eds. *Presidential Speechwriting: From the New Deal to the Reagan Revolution and Beyond.* College Station: Texas A & M University Press, 2003.

Russell, Peter. *Waking Up in Time: Finding Inner Peace in Times of Accelerating Change.* San Rafael, Calif.: Origin Press, 1998.

Senge, Peter. *The Fifth Discipline: The Art and Practice of the Learning Organization.* New York: Doubleday Currency, 1990.

Sharif, Abdullah. *Creating a World That Works For All.* San Francisco: Berrett-Koehler, 1999.

Smith, Huston. *The World's Religions: Our Great Wisdom Traditions.* San Francisco: HarperSanFrancisco,1994.

Solomon, Robert, and Fernando Flores. *Building Trust: In Business, Politics, Relationships, and Life.* Oxford: Oxford University, 2001.

Tannen, Deborah. *The Argument Culture: Moving from Debate to Dialogue.* New York: Random House, 1998.

Teilhard de Chardin, Pierre. *The Phenomenon of Man.* New York: Harper & Row, 1959.

Tocqueville, Alexis de. *Democracy in America.* New York: A. A. Knopf, 1945.

Twist, Lynne. *The Soul of Money: Transforming Your Relationship with Money and Life.* New York: W.W. Norton & Co., 2003.

Visser, Frank. Ken Wilber: *Thought as Passion.* Albany, N.Y.: State University of New York Press, 2003.

Walsh, Roger. *Essential Spirituality: The 7 Essential Practices to Awaken Heart and Mind.* Hoboken, N.J.: John Wiley & Sons, 1999.

Wheatley, Margaret. *Leadership and the New Science: Discovering Order in a Chaotic World.* San Francisco: Berrett-Koehler, 1999.

Whitworth, Laura. *Co-Active Coaching: New Skills for Coaching People Toward Success in Work and Life.* Palo Alto, Calif.: Davies-Black Publishing, 1998.

Wilber, Ken. *A Theory of Everything: An Integral Vision for Business*, Politics, Science and Spirituality. Boston: Shambala, 2001.

Williamson, Marianne, ed. *Imagine: What America Could Be in the 21st Century.* New York: New American Library, 2000.

Womeldorff, David. *Creating Sustainable Change: Seven Agreements for Accelerating Collaboration.* 2004. Unpublished Manuscript.

Zander, Rosamund and Benjamin. *The Art of Possibility.* Boston: Harvard Business School Press, 2000.

Zuck, Colleen, ed. *Unity Daily Word.* Unity Village, MO: Unity, April 2004.

A

B

C

Order Form

The Politics of Hope:
Reviving the Dream of Democracy

Order by Phone: Call 206.780.9900
Order by Mail: Politics of Hope
                  c/o Donna Zajonc
                  321 High School Road
                  Bainbridge Island, WA 98110
                  Fax 206-842-0296

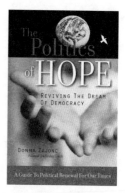

Order Online with PayPal at www.PoliticsofHope.com.

Qty	Title	Price	Can. Price	Total
	The Politics of Hope by Donna Zajonc	$16.95	$22.95	
Shipping & Handling in US: Add $3.95 + .50 each additional book				
Sales Tax (WA state residents only, add 8.9%)				
Total Enclosed				
Method of Payment ○ Visa ○ MasterCard ○ Check or money order enclosed				

_ _ _ _ _ _ _ _ _ _ _ _ _ _ _ _ _ _   _ _ _ / _ _ _

Card Number   Exp. Date

Signature _____

Name _____

Address_____

City_____State____Zip _____

Phone (___)_____Fax (___)_____

Email _____

Quantity discounts available. Thank you for your order!

For more information on programs, seminars,
and products from the Politics of Hope:

Public Speaking and Keynote Presentations
by Donna Zajonc
Political Leadership Coaching
Seminars and Consulting with individuals,
all levels of government, and non-profits
CDs and book orders

go to www.PoliticsofHope.com
or contact us by mail:

The Politics of Hope
Donna Zajonc
321 High School Road, Suite 295
Bainbridge Island, Washington 98110
Phone 206.780.9900
Fax 206.842.0296